Rosa Fairfax Costley

Fantasma

And Other Poems

Rosa Fairfax Costley

Fantasma
And Other Poems

ISBN/EAN: 9783744709859

Printed in Europe, USA, Canada, Australia, Japan

Cover: Foto ©Thomas Meinert / pixelio.de

More available books at **www.hansebooks.com**

FANTASMA

AND OTHER POEMS.

KANSAS CITY, MO.:
RAMSEY, MILLETT & HUDSON.
1879.

CONTENTS.

FANTASMA.
- Preface 7
- Characters of the Story 8
- Part First 9
- Part Second 26
- Part Third 44
- Part Fourth 94
- Part Fifth 114
- Notes 139

THE LIGHT-BRINGER.
- Preface 145
- Proem 147
- Part First 160
- Notes 198

MARCELLA.
- Introduction 203
- Canto I 205
- Canto II 218
- Canto III 240
- Notes 262

WILD IRIS AND OTHER RHYMES.

Wild Iris	269
The River	270
To My Brother	271
Amid the Corn	273
Ellen	275
The Lilly Queen	276
To Alice: A Reverie	281
Elizabeth Barrett Browning	284
The Silk Tree	286
In Darkness and the shadow of Death	287
Music in the Night	289
One in Ten	292
Indian Summer	294
A Comparison	295
Discontent	296
Fannie	298
Fidelity	299
My Brother	300
The Light of Other Days	301
Serenade	302
Rosa Senza Spinas	303
The Fairy Ring	304
The Jewel-Seeker	309
The Mocking-bird	311

FANTASMA:

A FAIRY TALE, IN FIVE PARTS.

When I goe musing all alone,
Thinking of diverse things foreknowne,
When I builde castles in the ayre,
Voide of sorrow, voide of fear,
Pleasing myself with fantasms sweete,
Methinks the time runnes very fleete.
—BURTON.

PREFACE.

TO ALICE.

O well-beloved! whose heart, in other days,
   Beat to my own with full-responsive chime,
   When our young pulses thrilled to sounds sublime
Of the Great Singer's world-entrancing lays;—
Thou, who didst walk with me the woodland ways
   Of fair Virginia, harkening, many a time,
   My childish fancies clothed in simplest rhyme,
Crowning the youthful poet with thy praise—
   Receive this scroll, wherein the verse appears
Of recent days: and, if it seems too light,
   Lacking the salt and bitter strength of tears,—
It is, that rose-winged Time has grown so bright,
And Faith has crowned, with blessings infinite,
   The joys and sorrows of my later years.

ROCKINGHAM COUNTY, N. C., August 15, 1876.

CHARACTERS OF THE STORY:

MORTALS.

BEAUCLERC, a Magician.
FLORIAN, a Poet.
DAN, Florian's Servant.
THE HERMIT.
  Witches, Wizards, etc.
LUCIA, the Sister of Florian.

FAIRIES, SPIRITS, ETC.

FANTASMA, Queen of all Fairies.
ROSEMARY, a Changeling.
EGLANTINE, the Fairy of Poesy.
LIGEIA, Queen of Sea-Nymphs.
ETHERIA Queen of the Sylphides.
AUREOLE, King of Fire-Sprites.
LAVENDER, a Changeling.
PHANTASM OF A POET.
  Fairies, Brownies, Fauns,
      Nymphs, etc.
  Evil Spirits and Familiars.

FANTASMA.

PART FIRST.

SCENE I.—*A lonely road through a Forest; a deserted Church.*

BEAUCLERC *enters, from the Wood.*

BEAUCLERC.

The evening shadows thicken in the woods,
And silence reigns in these dim solitudes,
Night-peopled by wild sprite and glimmering ghost,
And darker earthly shapes, with souls more lost.
This night, whose first sweet shades are here at last,
Will make amends for all my wretched past;
This thrice-blest night, that brings the fated hour
When fortune pours for me her golden shower,
Crowns me with love, and sceptres me with power!
                       [*A whippowil cries.*[1]
The signal-bird, calling the wood-sprites all
To keep to-night the full-moon festival,
Bids me take up yon fatal bough, that lies

On the worn steps that to the church-door rise—
A pledge of help in this night's enterprise.
                [*Takes up a spray of mistletoe.*
What lovely maid is this, abroad so late?
   Enter FANTASMA, *like a young girl, richly attired.*
Too bright a bird are you, to lack a mate—

FANTASMA.

Wound not with ribald speech a spirit's ear!
Unholy words are not for me to hear.
I am a spirit whom thou long didst seek
To bind with spells. Ah, mortal worse than weak!
Think'st thou, the soul of beauty can be thine?
Thou, less than man, *I*, child of the Divine?
Yet, I would warn thee; thou dost hope this night
To set the wrong above the unchampioned right.
Ah, blinded mortal, that shall never be!
Thou hast a foe—a powerful foe—in me!

BEAUCLERC.

Divine Fantasma! wilt thou ever be
The untiring foe of him who worships thee?
Take hands with me! this enmity forego—
To knowledge why should beauty be a foe?
Rouse from thy worship of a false Ideal,
And I will teach thee how to know the Real!
The bondage thou dost call religion, leave,
And the pure light of liberty receive.

From Faith's insane delusions wert thou free,
Freedom herself were proud to follow thee!

FANTASMA.

He who of Liberty so loudly raves
Is to his goddess bound, a slave of slaves,
To Freedom-and-Equality poor thrall—
Equality, the tyrant worst of all!
Alas! what madness in that dream must be
Of all impossible equality!
There *is* no freedom—heed the truth I speak—
There *is* no freedom, such as you would seek!
Neither in spirit-realm nor world of sense
Is freedom found: the law of consequence,
Alone, has forged a chain that will not break.
O hear and heed this truth for your own sake!
In the wide universe there is but ONE
Who is, or can be, free—for He alone
Is Strength and Love and Wisdom.—Child of clay!
Man's nature is, to trust, and to obey!
Vainly against this law wouldst thou rebel:
Servant of heaven, or else the slave of hell!

BEAUCLERC.

Spirit of loveliness! I take thy warning!
I give thee hate for hate and scorn for scorning!
I woo'd thee long, Fantasma the divine!
Henceforth, I am thy foe, as thou art mine.

Thou wild and frolic daughter of the woods,
The pet of Nature in her lightest moods,
With music-breathing lips and starlit eyes,
Untutored in earth's darker mysteries—
Thou succor the oppressed? *Thou* right the wrong?
Such deeds are not for thee, soft queen of song!

FANTASMA.

Vain mortal! I could almost pity thee.
Show but one touch of true humanity,
One gleam of mercy, and I yet will spare—
Will *save* thee from the doom that thou dost dare!

BEAUCLERC.

Thou spare? What strength from beauty can proceed,
Light as the wind, weak as a trembling reed?
Know, lovely phantom of the shining brow,
I deal with spirits mightier far than thou,
Before whose flames thy firefly light would fade,
And thou shrink to the shadow of a shade!
[*The church windows shine from light within. Wild music.*
But, hark, the signal! Dare not thou, this night,
A mortal, armed in more than mortal might!
Stronger than thy soft arm the power must be
That locks the rolling wheel of destiny.

[*He goes into the church.*

FANTASMA.

That power lies in the strength of purity!
It has been promised me that I shall find

FANTASMA.

A helper, pure of heart and strong of mind:
And, lo, the time is come, the steps draw near,
And youth, and strength, and purity are here!
And timid ignorance comes after him,
Trembling at moonlight shapes and shadows dim.

Enter FLORIAN *and* DAN.

FLORIAN.

Why, who is this fair girl, so late abroad,
In this dark forest, on so lone a road?

DAN.

Don't you go for to speak to her, Mas' Flo.!
She come from dat ole graveyard, what *you* know?
Dat ar ole church is haunted anyhow.
When we was down de road a little ways,
I hearn de organ play, and seen de windows blaze.

FLORIAN.

Lady, what do you in this lonely wood?
They call it haunted, this dim solitude.

FANTASMA.

Sir, I have lost my way, and hither strayed;
And now, to turn or to advance afraid,
I trust your chivalry to give me aid.

FLORIAN.

So far as I have power, I pledge my word

To aid you to the utmost, till restored
To your own home, wherever that may be.

FANTASMA.

You pledge your word to this?

FLORIAN.

      Most full and free!

FANTASMA.

I take the pledge! Before the morning's light
You must redeem it as a faithful knight.
Farewell—but ere the midnight hour shall fade,
I summon thee to give the promised aid!
                [*She disappears.*

DAN.

Dar, now! what does you think o' dat, Mas' Flo.?
I knowed she was a witch; I tole you so!

FLORIAN.

'Tis more than strange, indeed! I well might deem
That figure but the illusion of a dream.

DAN.

O lord! What made you come dis way to-night?
We'll be forever ha'nted by dat sprite!

FLORIAN.

Why should you tremble with such needless fear?
It was a most gentle ghost that met us here,

(If ghost it be), and a most lovely one:
A fairer face I never looked upon!
You should be more astonished than afraid
At this, the wild trick of some country maid.

DAN.

"Trick?" Yes, will bofe be tricked,[2] dat's mighty clear!
Is you bewitched, to stand a-gazin' here!
Come on, Mas' Flo., and less git out o' dis.
Come on; come on; I'm gwine for home, *I* is!

SCENE II.—*A wild glade in the Forest.*

Enter ROSEMARY, JACK-O-LANTERN, *and Fairies.*

FIRST FAIRY.

I float upon the thistledown,
  That light and merry rover!
The west-wind is my wingèd steed
  To bear me far away,
Above the tumult of the town,
  The deep-green country over!
More useful things may be, indeed,
  But few so light. and gay!

SECOND FAIRY.

I lead the train of lightning-flies
    That twinkle in the twilight!
I wake the lilies from their dreams;
    The roses all unfold;
The tulips flaunt their brilliant dyes
    Beneath my flashing fly-light;
And the lightly-drooping fuchsia seems
    A fount of starry gold!

JACK-O-LANTERN.

The bonny elfin-fire am I,
    That glimmers in the gloaming!
The meadow-fays dance merrily
    Beneath my fitful gleam;
The forest-fairies follow me,
    For all my willful roaming,
Beneath my dancing light to see
    Their faces in the stream!

The lurking thief starts back to see
    My rays beside him glancing!
Benighted men do I mislead,
    And wile them from their way!
The merry wildfire flickers free,
    O'er marsh and meadow dancing—
Far truer lights there are, indeed,
    But none so wild and gay!

ROSEMARY.

Have you performed your task, and led astray
Young Florian to the forest?

JACK-O-LANTERN.
     Far away
From their true path I led them; and full soon
They will be here, wild-wandering by the moon.
Was it well done, Rosemary?

ROSEMARY.
     Truly, yes,—
But now it is mine hour of heaviness,
When I my senses in light slumber steep:
The air-born fairies on the wing may sleep,
But I am but a changeling fay, at best,
And slumber bows my head to the green breast
Of earth, my mother, where I take my rest.
Upon this bed of wood-moss I will lie
Till time shall bring the wandering Florian nigh,
Whose coming must arouse me. Quickly run,
Light fairies! Tell our queen the task is done.
[*She sleeps.* JACK-O-LANTERN *and the Fairies flit away.*

Enter FLORIAN *and* DAN.

DAN.

Well, if I *does* git outen dis, yere wood,

I'll just stay outen hit forebber mo!
O massy-sakes-alive! What *is* dis yere?

FLORIAN.

What is it, now? A child, and quite alone!
What.chance is this, within the forest wild?
Who and whence art thou, lone and lovely child?

ROSEMARY.

Rosemary, I am called. I've lost my way.

DAN.

Dat's jest what all the pesky goblins say.

FLORIAN.

Dan, go you now to yonder ruddy light
That gleams so brightly from that distant height;
'Tis, doubtless, some lone house upon the hill,
Or, haply, it may shine from Barksdale's mill—
The ruined mill, where the good hermit lives:
All—wandering, lost, or homeless—he receives.
Whate'er it is, go, seek that light and say
How we in this dim forest lost our way,
And, therefore, ask for shelter, rest and food
For us and this young child, lost in the wood.

DAN.

De debil fetch me, if I stirs dis night
To follow any Jack-ma-Lanter's[2] light!

Has you forgot when we fust lost de road,
How like a lamp de Jack-ma-Lanter glowed?
You said de light was in some house you knowed.
And den we followed dat deceitful fire
Till I went plump into de black marsh-mire,
And waist-deep in de mud an' rushes stuck,
An' flopped an' floundered like a hurt wild-duck;
An' when I scrambled out, we bofe turned back,
But, in de dark, of course, we lost de track.
And somethin' come behind me wid a push,
And pitched me headlong in a blackberry bush;
And dis here nigger's skin got more'n one scratch
'Fore he got outen dat ole blackberry patch.
And somethin' poked me awful in de ribs,
And bofe my eyes was full of spider-webs;
I hit a stump an' gin. my shins a rake,
An' pretty nigh stepped on a moc'sin snake,
An', last, I tumbled in de brook down yonder:
An' ain't all this enough for onct, I wonder?
Now, you must send me deeper in de wood
To find dat light, shinin' from thick marsh-mud,
Or risin' from some still, black, shiny pool,
Or quakin' quicksand. Think ole Dan's a fool?
I haint a-gwine to quit you till we go,
Bofe of us, outen dis here woods, Mas' Flo.!

FLORIAN.

What, will you play the coward? Yonder light

Is no wildfire; it glimmers from a height.
There's neither marsh nor quicksand on a hill;
That is some house, or else 'tis Barksdale's mill,
Built where the stream leaps to the lake below.
Shake off your childish fears, good Dan, and go!
Till you return, I will not quit this place.

Dan.

Nor *I* shant leave it, neither—here I stays
Till I git out o' here by broad daylight.
De ghosts haint pestered *you* dis livelong night;
But dere's a difference twixt us two, you see;
De ghosts an' goblins has a spite at me,
An' till I fetch my head safe out o dis,
I gwine to stick right close to *you*, *I* is!

Florian.

Then, take the child, and I will lead the way.
What now, sir? Will you neither go nor stay?

Dan.

I haint a-gwine to tetch dat chile, Mas' Flo.!
If taint a goblin hit's de debil, sho'!
Why don't she cry, as nat'rally she would
If 'twas a human chile lost in de wood?
Look at her frock, as green as meadow-grass,
And shiny all like specks of isin'-glass;
Dem tangled curls is all in elf-locks tied—
An' jest look at de creeter's eyes! how wide

An' full of mischief! black an' shiny, too,
As new-ripe chinquapins all wet wid dew!
And, now, above her forehead, what's dat ar?
Dat greenish light, a-tremblin' like a star—
Pale fire, dat looks so like a fadin' spark,
Same as de fox-fire,[2] shinin' in de dark?

FLORIAN.

Most strange and beautiful! What may this be?
Fair child, what art thou?

ROSEMARY.

I am Rosemary.

DAN.

Tell *you*, you better drop dat chile, Mas' Flo.!
She hang you wid a grape-vine, fust you know,
Or strangle you wid a young hazel-switch:
For, if she ain't de debil, she's a witch.

FLORIAN.

Dan, listen! you must either quickly go
And find what is the light that's gleaming so,
Or I shall go! I have no mind to stay
Within this forest till the dawn of day.
I know not why you feel so much alarm;
Thus far, the ghosts have done us little harm.

DAN.

Well, ef I mus', I mus': I'm 'tween two fires;
I mus' go chasin' through de brush and briers

Follerin' Jack-ma-Lanters, till I'm lost,
Or stay here wid dat chile; and hit's a ghost.
I'd jest as lief to go as stay, Mas' Flo.,
For I'm afear'd either to stay or go.
Don't quit dis place, Mas' Flo., de debil's in it
If you don't see me back in half a minute!

[*Exit.*

ROSEMARY.

Yes, Florian! Dan is right! Poor ignorance
Stumbles on knowledge, by some guess or chance,
Which culture misses.

FLORIAN.

You are not a ghost,
Or elf, sweet child?

ROSEMARY.

A changeling elf, at most;
A fairy child who loves the human kind.
To mischief much, to mirth much more inclined.
I can, upon occasion, put away
Mischief and merriment. A household fay
Am I; and therefore did the fairy queen
Send me to be your guide—perhaps, your screen.

FLORIAN.

Sweet wonder! Wherefore sent your queen to me?
What service to a fairy can there be
In my bewildered wandering in this wood?

FANTASMA.

ROSEMARY.

Ah, heretofore you have not understood.
To-night, the witches hold their carnival,
And a lost mortal, Satan's willing thrall,
Will join them—not, indeed, to share their sport;
He follows evil of a higher sort.
There is a spirit-life, whose subtle thread
Links the blind living to the enlightened dead,
And in its viewless windings, fold on fold,
Sphere within sphere, it doth creation hold;—
The soul of the material universe,
To which the eye of science cannot pierce,
Nor reason demonstrate the *how* and *why*
Of this, the Great Supreme's unuttered mystery.
Sometimes, as though in mockery of the wise,
The gates unclose to Superstition's eyes,
But Ignorance stops, the threshold barely crossed,
Trembling before a spectre or a ghost.
But there are minds of a far higher sort,
Yet lower, who the powers of darkness court
For gain or glory, and with demons hold
Converse, and so win pleasure, power or gold.
Such scruple not to fling their souls away
For the vain pageant of an earthly day.
A soul may be so dark, so steeped in sense,
It flies from light as from a pestilence,
And, could it to the gates of heaven be sent,
Would seek hell, as a lighter punishment.

Such were the powerful Magians of the eld,
Who with the dead unhallowed converse held;
And such a soul, although far less in power,
Pollutes our grove in this, the witches' hour.

FLORIAN.

But what is this unhappy man to me?
Can I, then, win him from his infamy?

ROSEMARY.

Not so; but you can from like evil save
A soul which he will otherwise enslave,—
A maiden-spirit, beautiful and rare,
White as a snowflake in the moonlit air;
Yet this man seeks her for a fatal power,
A fairy-gift, and a most perilous dower—
Clear-visioned soul and spirit-quickened eyes
That pierce the veil of hidden mysteries.
Whoever weds her, in that very hour
The quickened sight is his, with doubled power;
But, if her love to this dark soul is given,
The maid is lost at once to earth and heaven.
Prevent this fatal marriage! for it lies
With you to slay or save the sacrifice!

FLORIAN.

Fairy! From childhood even to this night
My dreams have still been blessed with forms of light

Who breathed strange visions into my dim brain,
Heightened my bliss and soothed away my pain.
And, often in my musing solitude
In smiling lowlands or in bowery wood,
Glimpses I caught of forms unearthly fair,
And whispers thrilled the lulled and listening air
That promised me some unimagined bliss:
Surely, there is no greater joy than this,
To guard, to save, imperiled purity!
Such task the angels well might envy me!

ROSEMARY.

Come, then! The sorcerer a spell has laid
Upon this hapless and most innocent maid,
That holds her in deep sleep. In her own room
She lies, beneath the sheltering roof of home,
Yet, ere the midnight passes, they will bring
The enchanted maiden to the witches' ring.
In such a contest, fairies are but weak,
And yet we have much power. From you we seek
The matchless strength of faith and purity;
What more is needed, we can well supply.
Victory in this is for the pure in heart,
The gentle, faithful, brave: and such thou art!

PART SECOND.

SCENE I.—*The level Uplands overlooking a Lake in the Wood. Voices in the air of Unseen Spirits.*

        FIRST VOICE.
Come away! come away!

        SECOND VOICE.
    Haste, oh! haste! No longer stay!

        FIRST VOICE.
For the midnight hour is fleeting
Which should see our joyous meeting.

        SECOND VOICE.
Magic dews are softly falling;

        FIRST VOICE.
Your familiar spirits calling;

        SECOND VOICE.
Nightshade here is rankly growing;

        FIRST VOICE.
Hemlock deepest shadow throwing;

SECOND VOICE.
Here the wreathed snake is tracing;

FIRST VOICE.
Venomed laurels interlacing;

SECOND VOICE.
Deadly blooms their leaves unfurling;

FIRST VOICE.
Vapors from the marsh up-curling;

SECOND VOICE.
Here the shades of night come quickly;

FIRST VOICE.
Here the rankest weeds grow thickly;

SECOND VOICE.
Here the muffled owl is sitting;

FIRST VOICE.
Here the leathern bats are flitting;

SECOND VOICE.
Here the shriveled toad is leaping; .

FIRST VOICE.
Poison-vines are thickly creeping;

SECOND VOICE.
Earth's untold and hideous evils
Here are hoarded for your revels.

FIRST VOICE.
Ere the blooms of midnight wither,
Daughters of the Night, come hither!

SECOND VOICE.
While the dews of midnight glitter
On the nightshade black and bitter,
Sons of Darkness, do not stay!

BOTH VOICES.
Come away! come away!

Enter WITCHES *and* WIZARDS; *to them*, BEAUCLERC.

BEAUCLERC.
Ah, wild and wicked wanderers of the night!
Our circle now is rounded and complete
In number as the still and charmèd hour
Wherein gray morning clasps the hand of night.

FIRST WITCH.
Welcome! most welcome.

FIRST WIZARD.
Wherefore are you late?

SECOND WIZARD.
Where is the maiden you should bring with you?

BEAUCLERC.
Be patient, all. —Ye know the ruined mill
And the gray hermit dwelling there?

FIRST VOICE.
      Indeed,
We know him, and with reason.

BEAUCLERC.
      He, our foe,
Whom even the harmless wood-sprites fear and shun,
He must be cast into profoundest sleep,
Or else removed from the enchanted wood;
His presence here is fatal to our power,
For he is one of those born torturers
Who think to win that fabled heaven of theirs,
(Hard as their hearts and narrow as their creed,)
By making hell of earth. He, from the world
Flying, because no worship now is paid
To priests or kings as in the earth's young years,
Dwells in this wood, a lonely self-tormentor,
Vexing free nature with his prayers and groans.
I say, this dotard's tongue must be kept still;
Ay, even all thought be banished from his brain,
Or our familiars lose their wonted power.

First Witch.

Let two of us cast on him that strong spell
That bound young Lucia. It has never failed.

Beauclerc.

Yes, go, and put the powerful charm to proof;
But venture not beneath the hermit's roof.
Remember, if he should awake, our pain
Is profitless; our invocations vain.
        [*Exit 1st Witch and 1st Wizard.*

Haste we to brighten this wild forest's gloom
With beauty in its full and perfect bloom.

    Spirits to my bidding rise;
      Spirits, beautiful and free,
    Hasten to the place where lies
      The maiden, sleeping dreamlessly.
    Thither, on untiring wing
      Through the shades of midnight sweep;
    Sweep, with speed of thought, and bring
      The maiden in her charmed sleep.

Two beautiful Demons *descend, bearing* Lucia, *asleep, veiled, and crowned with poppies. They place her in the midst of the Circle.*

SECOND WIZARD.
O Beautiful!

THIRD WIZARD.
Most lovely, if the face
Is half so fair as that exquisite form.

SECOND WITCH.
But wherefore does she wear that shining veil,
And wreath of poppies, crimson and milkwhite?

BEAUCLERC.
That garland brings forgetfulness; that veil—
While shrouded in that veil, no voice but mine
Has power to break her deep, entrancèd sleep.
The hour is waning; join ye hand in hand;
When she awakens, she will soulless be
And mindless, as unconscious infancy.

CHANT.
By the strong, unhallowed power
  Which is ours, in this wild hour,
We, the ministers of hell,
  Break thy magic garland's spell.
Ere the witches' circle break,
  Maiden, from thy sleep awake;
Ere the hour of midnight flies,
  Maiden, from thy trance arise!

LUCIA *awakes and stands in the midst of the Ring.*

BEAUCLERC (*to the witches, etc.*)
Assume whatever shape best pleases you,
To wait upon our Master, who, to-night
Will join our revels at the ruined church.
Then, till the dawning day, ye all have power
To work your wills, so that you do no good.

THIRD WITCH.
I'll take the bright form of a humming bird,
And (service to our Master done) will flit
Through the spice-breathing groves of Florida.

SECOND WIZARD.
I, like a spotted snake, will coil in weeds,
And strike the unwary who shall pass thereby.

BEAUCLERC.
Lucia, the stars are on the lake;
 Come, draw your veil aside,
That hides the liquid light of eyes
 Softer than any star that lies
  Upon the trembling tide.

The silver-rippling waves that break
 Along the willowed shore,
Sing like the music memories make
 Of dreaming days of yore.
But speak! The sighing wind will hush,
 The listening lake lie still,

And mocking-bird and tender thrush,[1]
Be silent on the hill!

LUCIA.

O beautiful, new world! How strangely fair;
Could I not float upon the soft night air,
Or dance upon the shining lake afar,
Like the reflection of that lovely star?

FOURTH WITCH.

The night-wind rushes, wild and free,
   Down from the distant river!
The wayward wind, so fresh and free,
   So fetterless and light!
O would that I those winds could be,
   And rove the world forever,
With none to curb or question me;
   With none to doubt my right.

(*A strain of wild and melancholy music.*)

BEAUCLERC.

Lucia, draw close your veil about your face,
An enemy approaches—*what*, I know not,
Or mortal, or a spirit of the wood.

Enter FLORIAN; ROSEMARY *follows, invisible.*

Depart! and take our novice hence with you

(*Witches and Wizards ascend with Lucia and vanish.*)

Who are you, that durst break the witches' ring?
You are not mortal; else you have the aid
Of those who are not!

Florian.
    O thou vile magician!
Where is the maid whom thy inhuman art
Has blinded and beguiled? Be sure of this,
That from this forest thou shalt not depart
Till thou hast freed her from thy cruel spells.

Beauclerc.
A face too girlish for a tongue so bold!
I know thee well, although thou knowest not me,
Fair youth; I'll try the power of that same art
On thee, who durst so rudely challenge me.
I charge thee, by this rod, and by its power,
And by the Power that gives its magic strength—
Stir not, nor leave the spot whereon thou standest,
Till I release and tell thee to depart!

Florian.
I laugh thee and thy power to scorn! Thou seest,
I move; and I will try another power;
The strength that Nature gave me.—This is strange!
Something repels me, when I would approach;
Yet he had not the power to fetter me!

Rosemary (*appearing*).

Forbear! He has no power on you, indeed,
Nor have you power on him.
The weight of good and evil balance here.

Florian.

That may not be, for Goodness is Supreme.
If I but trusted in my own weak arm,
I were already vanquished.

Beauclerc.

    So thou art!
I know thee, and the power that is thy friend.
A dewdrop shall the red volcano quench
When thou and thine shall conquer mine or me!
           [*Exit.*

Florian.

And yet, he flies! Nay, I will follow him!
Fairy, think not to turn or stay me, now.

Rosemary.

But you must hear me! I have disobeyed
The fairy-queen's commands to bring you here;
She bade me lead you to her woodland bower.
This man is shielded by a dreadful Power;
And, Florian, good can never spring from ill;
Success comes not to disobedience.
Turn not away, nor bend impatient brows,
For haste is still the parent of defeat,

And I have sinned, in that I disobeyed,
For sin and disobedience are one.

FLORIAN.

Then haste we to your queen Fantasma's bower.

[*Exeunt.*

SCENE II. *Before the Hermit's Mill on the edge of the wood.*

Enter DAN.

DAN.

Well, here I is, at las', and dars de light
Dat brought me here. Dis time Mas' Flo. was right;
Hits in de mill; de ole man's still awake.
I'll knock, and gin de do' a little shake
To make him come de quicker. (*Knocks.*) I jes' feels
As ef a dozen ghosts was at my heels.
A nigger better be uncommon good
Dat walks at midnight through dis fetched wood.
Dis nigger'll never pester hit no mo,'
Ef he gits outen it *dis* time, dat's sho'!

[*Knocks.*

Ole man! Ole man! Come, open dis here do'!

Enter from the Mill, the HERMIT.

HERMIT.

Who or what is it, visits me so late?

DAN.

Hits me, Sir—Dan. You know me, Sir?

HERMIT.

I think,
Indeed, I know you. Whither do you go,
And whence come you, at this untimely hour?

DAN.

I hain't abroad on my own business, Mahs';
Niggers don't roam so late widout a pass,
And, if dey does, dey don't make midnight ja'nts
Through lonesome woods dat's all alive wid ha'nts.

HERMIT.

Tell me, in brief; stand you in need of help,
Of food or lodging for the night? Your wants,
In either case, I gladly will supply,
For, 'tis my duty, no less than my pleasure,
To succor all who stand in need of help,
And aid them to the limit of my power.

DAN.

Me and Mas' Flo., we done got los', *we* is,
Fol'rin' a Jack-ma-lanter' through de woods.

HERMIT.

Hither, then, bring your master, whom I know.
And any who may be with him. Return,

Nor stand thus idly, lest they further stray,
And lose themselves yet deeper in the wood.

Dan.

O! Sir, for pity's sake, don't send me back,
Or, (if you does), go wid me! Hits a fac',
In daylight, I'm as brave as any man,
But, dis here night has been too much for Dan;
Jack-o'-ma-lanters, fust, and den a witch;
And now, de night's done turned as black as pitch,
Like as a storm was comin'. Sir, I know
Dere's witches in dese woods—it's sartain, sho'!
If *I* goes back, for goodness sake, *you* go!

Hermit.

I do not scorn your natural fear, good Dan;
Long have I dwelt within the forest here,
And many wondrous things have pondered on,—
Things that the wisest cannot all explain.
Yet, this believe; that darkness shuns the light,
And evil, boldly faced, from goodness flies.
It is the guilt of our own conscious hearts,
And not our enemy, that conquers us.

Dan.

I know it, Mas', and I been awful mean!
But, if you can't go wid me, I'll go back,
Ruther than leave Mas' Flo.; for goodness knows
What's come o' him and dat ar goblin chile.

Hermit.

Why, now you speak right manly! I will go
Into the wood with you. The impending storm
Will, as I think, last but a little while,
Yet threatens to be violent.—Tell me, Dan,
What mean you, talking of a goblin child?

Dan.

Why, hits a witch, Sir, as I said befo'.
We found her sleepin' in de wood. Mas' Flo.,
Who don't mind nothin' 'tall 'bout ghosts and sich,
He wouldn't b'live de pretty thing's a witch.
[*Thunder.*

Hermit.

Stand close, good Dan. There's evil in the air,
And danger threatens me. Nay, tremble not!
We are shielded by the overruling Goodness.
Stand silent in the shade, and have no fear.
Enter Witch *and* Wizard.

Wizard.

Come, let us lose no time! Night wears away.

Witch.

I almost fear to practice on this man.
I tremble, when by some unhappy chance
I meet him in my walks about the wood,
And shrink away from meeting his strong eye.
I even fear the light that falls upon

His reverend beard and silver hair unshorn.
What if the charm should fail?

WIZARD.

It never fails,
For all the powers of air have given it strength.
Did it not bind young Lucia? Who more pure
Or more devout than she? And yet she lies
Helpless beneath the power of this strong spell.

WITCH.

Well, speak it then! The thronging demons wait.

INVOCATION.

Hither, ye spirits of enchanted sleep,
              Hither, sweep!
On winds that shake the moaning pines, and wake
The rising waves of the darkening lake!
Come! In the drowsy fogs that slowly creep
             From the marshy brake!
Whatever spells ye keep of silence or of sleep
Pour on the troubled air till dumbness conquers prayer,
And no vain dreamings of impossible good
Disturb our revels in the haunted wood!
          · Hermit, sleep!
Sleep! We have bound thee, body, soul and brain!
Sleep soundly, profoundly, nor waken again,
Till we have unbound thee, and loosened the chain
Wherein we have wound thee, soul, body and brain.

Enter another WIZARD.

SECOND WIZARD.

Say, is it done?

FIRST WIZARD.

'Tis done, and thoroughly!
If spells can bind, he will not wake to-night.

SECOND WIZARD.

Haste, then, to join us at the ruined church,
Where our dark Master leads the revelry.
We need his aid, for most inopportune,
Strange and unlooked for interruption came
To our wild circle, at the very height
Of joy, and every promise of success.
Scarcely Beauclerc had waked the sleeping maid,
When the rash youth, young Florian, burst upon us,
Set on and aided by the fairy queen,
In hope to snatch from us the valued prize.
Beauclerc withstood the fairy-favored youth,
And we bore off the prize, our trancèd girl;
And I am sent to bid ye come with haste
To the old church. She must be one of us,
At any cost, and with all speed. The storm
[*Thunder.*
Whose darkness adds new terror to the wood
Will rid us of the meddling fairy-crew,
Our flimsy foes; they fly from the wild strife

Of the warring elements to fairy-land.
These, and the Hermit, only need we fear.
The Hermit ye have chained; an enemy
Right formidable; but the unstable fays
Are little to be dreaded. Even their queen,
Fantasma of the shining brow, is weak,
Save in the wavering strength that beauty gives.
    [*Thunder and Lightning. A Storm.*

    First Wizard.
Despise not overmuch Fantasma's power.
Our Master has not raised this storm for naught.

    Witch.
Come, come, and let us hasten to the church!
We waste the night, which should be given to mirth.
 [*Storm continues. They rise and disappear singing:*
   Away, away, on the winds we fly,
   On fogs, that rise from the lake hard by;
   On flitting bat, and screeching owl,
   And clouds that on the landscape scowl!

    Hermit.
Thus have you been the instrument of heaven,
Good Dan, to save me from the witches' spell,
Perchance to save the maid of whom they spoke
And bright, young Florian.

Dan.

O my soul, dear Mas'.
I skeered so bad I dunno whar I is!
Let's go right on to dat ole church, and so
Find out what dey bin done wid po' Mas' Flo. !

Hermit.

First, seek the spot where you left Florian;
It must lie in direction of the church,
Since you have crossed the wood in coming here.
If Florian has, indeed, gone from the place,
Then we will seek the old, deserted church
Which they have desecrated with vile orgies.
Courage, and forward, Dan! Good must prevail!

PART THIRD.

SCENE I. *A Flowery Glen between Rocky Cliffs.* FANTASMA, *as the Fairy Queen, swinging in her hammock under a canopy of Grape and Muscadine.*[1] *Fauns and Fairies.*

FANTASMA.
The hour is past, and yet they do not come!
My eager eyes would pierce the moonless gloom
To meet those forms that yet do not appear.
Harm has befallen them, I sadly fear!
    Azalea, draw more near;
This crimson trumpet from the creeper take,
And sound a fairy peal, that echoes may awake;
So shall they catch the echoes as they fly,
    And hearing, make reply!
        [AZALEA *sounds a peal.*
The echoes die, and bring us no reply!

    LAVENDER, (*a fairy*).
O queen, Fantasma, at thy grief
The trembling dew slides, tear-like, from the leaf,
    The night-blooms weep,
And all the folded flowers awake from sleep,

And sadness falls upon the fairy crowd.
    Vain is thy fear!
Ere the full moon arises from the cloud,
    The wanderers will be here.

FANTASMA.

Where is the wildfire whose bewildering light
Drew Florian to the haunted wood to-night?
Lights dance through the forest; one approaches FANTASMA,
    borne by JACK-O-LANTERN.
Go, glancing Wildfire! and, within the hour,
Bring Florian and Rosemary to my bower.

JACK-O-LANTERN.

I flicker and fly, in the flash of an eye;
As the gleam of a star that shoots through the sky.
    [*He flits into the forest.*

FANTASMA.

Sweet Lavender, come near to me!
Thou and thy gentle sister Rosemary
Are not the least belovèd of thy queen,
Among those shapes that dance upon the green
Or sprinkle with fresh dews the grassy lea.
And let me hear thy voice most clear,
Sweet Eglantine, the soul of poesy;
    Whose bosom, in its gentle rise and fall,
Flutters the winglets of the butterfly
Which ever does in azure beauty lie

Upon thy breast, O thou most fair of all!
The lightest word thy honeyed lips let fall,
Nay, the least motion of thy soft light hair,
Fills with sweet murmurs the delighted air,
And wakes the wild glade's echoes musical.

EGLANTINE, (*a fairy*).

Come, fairies, cheer our queen with song and sport;
So shall the merry moments seem too short.

SONG.

Let the hammock lightly swing,
Like a bird upon the wing!
It is braided through and through
With willow-shoots and green bamboo;[2]
With lace-bark woven all across,
And filaments of long, gray moss;
Lined with humming-bird's rich plumes;
Wreathed about with ivy-blooms![3]
Rock our queen upon its bosom,
Like the fringe-tree's waving blossom;
Like an oriole in her nest,
Swan upon a river's breast,
Lily on a streamlet swinging,
Mocking-bird in moonlight singing![4]

FANTASMA.

Come, tell me, laughing faun and merry fay,
What hast thou done, to-night or yesterday?

Laurel, begin, sweet mountain sprite!
What task has thou performed, this night?

LAUREL, (*a fairy*).

I have been stringing berries red as coral,
    To twine thy long, bright hair,
And I have wreathed of my own mountain-laurel,
    A crown for thee to wear.

MORNING-GLORY, (*a fairy*).

This morning, I unfolded to the dew
    My tender blue,
And to the bluebird's glancing eye
I seemed a piece of summer sky,
    So like himself in hue
He could not pass me by;
So from his shining pinions he let fall
These azure plumes that deck my coronal.

WOODBINE,[5] (*a fairy*).

And what the bluebird did for thee
The beautiful wild redbird did for me,
And scattered from his scarlet breast
The fiery plumes that blaze upon my crest.
And what hast *thou* done, dark-eyed faun?

HAZEL, (*a faun*).

I caught the liquid gems of dawn,
    And sowed them thickly on the velvet moss

And wildflowers sweet,
And ferns, that line this valley all across,
To fit it for Fantasma's fairy feet.

SILVERLEAF, (*another faun*).
I found the wild cucumber-tree,[6]
And of its long leaves, two or three
I made into a cup as greenly bright
As costly chalice, carved of malachite;
Then filled it from the fountain's inner veins,
And mixed therewith the juice of sugar-canes,
And held it to the thin and pallid lip
Of a young child, who daily comes to dip
Her pitcher in the forest spring.
She is a sad and gentle thing;
But when she drank of my green cup to-day,
She brightly smiled, and lightly tripped away!

FANTASMA.
My gentle faun, thou hast done well, indeed!
To give what ease they may, to hearts that bleed,
To cheer the friendless, driving care away—
This is the sweetest task of faun or fay.

EGLANTINE.
A group of tall magnolia trees
I saw to-day, tossing upon the breeze
The waxen petals of their flowers full-blown;
In languid beauty softly floating down,

FANTASMA.

Like flying swans that lightly settle
Upon a forest lake, each broad, white petal
Fell, wavering to the grass. And then I ran
And chose one, large enough to be the fan
Perfumed and satin-shining that is swayed
By the fair fingers of a mortal maid,
And beautiful enough to be the screen
That shuts the moonlight from our own sweet queen.

FANTASMA.
            Eglantine, my sweet,
I see the dance makes light my elfins' feet;
Lead the light fairies in a lovely ring
Of dancers, gliding slow and circling fleet,
As dimpling eddies where two streamlets meet.
Let flute and voice be mingled as you sing.

SONG.
Magic dews of midnight glisten
  Through our fairy glen,
For the full moon has risen
  From the clouds again,
And her liquid light is glancing
  Through the flowery glade
Where our sister fays are dancing
  In the flickering shade.
The sweetest dews we'll gather up,
And fill with them the lily's cup,

To freshen lips that wasting grief
Has withered like an autumn leaf.

Here the shining ivy's drooping
   From the rocky wall;
Here the ash-tree's tassels stooping—
   Fairest tree of all!
Here the eglantine is flinging
   Fragrance through the groves;
Here the mocking-bird is singing
   In the light he loves.
We'll weave to-night a fairy wreath,
   And fairy dreams about it breathe,
And on sad, sleeping brows will lay,
   To banish cruel care away.

O'er the placid stream is bending
   The narcissus pale,
With the sweet-fern's odor blending
   Fragrance faint and frail;
The poppy sleeps, though light is sifting
   O'er her blossoms bright;
But the heartsease wakes, up-lifting
   Glad looks to the light.
We'll gather blossom, leaf, and stem,
And bind the almond-flower with them,
And place them on the troubled heart,
That peace may come and pain depart.

FANTASMA.
Cease, cease! The wildfire dances through the gloom;
I breathe the evanescent, faint perfume
From the green garland of sweet Rosemary;
And now, young Florian's own fair form I see!

Enter JACK-O-LANTERN, ROSEMARY *and* FLORIAN.

JACK-O-LANTERN.
I danced through the forest with sparkle and flicker;
Ever the forest grew thicker and thicker;
Ever my sparkle went quicker and quicker,
Until I had found them, and circling around them,
I led them once more as I led them before.

FLORIAN.
So many wonders have I seen to-night
Thy wondrous beauty dazzles not my sight,
O, seeming woman! O, most lovely shape,
Throned airily beneath thy bower of grape!
Crowned with a truly fairy coronet
Of trembling sensitive vines, all dewy wet,
With feathery foliage, blooms like tufted fringes,
Or downy globes with delicate pink tinges!
Sweet is the star that o'er thy forehead trembles;
Sweeter the eyes whose light that star resembles!
Enchanting vision, art thou witch or fairy?
Mortal, or bright dream of a visionary?

FANTASMA.

Look in my face more closely.   Dost thou see
Nothing that awakes a memory of me?

FLORIAN.

O, all too much!   From childhood to this day
Thy light divine has been around my way!
Thou soul of Beauty, lamp of my bright past,
Joy of the present, art thou mine at last?
And hast thou broken that fine mystery,
That like a crystal wall surrounded thee,
Through which I could not pass, yet could most clearly
    see?

FANTASMA.

Not yet, not yet has come the happy day
When that bright wall shall melt like mist away,
And spirit walk dismantled of its clay!
But, Florian, from thy happy past recall
One hour that seems to thee the best of all—
The hour of perfect bliss, whatever it be,
Recall it in its almost witchery.

FLORIAN.

All the buried hours, arising at thy call, embodied came,
Flashing by in long-lost brightness, like a sudden burst of
    flame;
But of all the hours, Fantasma, that awoke at memory's call,
One there is, by far the brightest and the best among them all.

I was in the earliest childhood that is conscious of a soul;
And the sweet waves of existence came and went with silver roll,
Bringing to us childish treasures: for I did not walk alone:
Hand in hand with me went ever my twin-sister: two in one,
Moved our spirits, softly blended: in that hour, whose glory now
Shines about me, we together took *thy* sign upon the brow!

We were at an open window, looking out upon the night,
On the deep and solemn heavens, flooded with the trancing light
Of the mystic moon, whose silence lay on all things like a spell;
Even the mocking-bird was silent; only, with a softened swell,
Came the murmur of the river, flowing, ever flowing down
From the heart of azure mountains curving past the lovely town,
Winding through the fringing willows, past the greenly rising hills;
Blooming spice along its borders all the air with fragrance fills:
It was early spring, but milder than it sometimes is in May;
Though the grass was thickly springing, here and there the snow-wreaths lay.

Thawing ice upon the terrace sparkled with pale, pearly hue;
Faint, sweet odors came and told us where the wild arbutus grew,

And the violet's stronger fragrance rose like incense to the moon:
Chilly March a night had stolen from the glowing month of June.

Then the mocking-bird, whose silence had drunk melody like wine,
Poured for us a song whose sweetness only could be matched with thine!
For, in thy supernal beauty, thou didst stand before us there—
Not so rich the moon's white glory, not so sweet the flowing air!
At thy touch the waking spirit saw the Earth before it lie,
In her beauty and her glory, in her heaven-taught melody!
And of happy hours and shining that awake at memory's call,
That to me is still the brightest and the best among them all!

Fantasma.

This night shall bring thee all I promised thee,
If thou art worthy to be loved of me;
But thou must not be lightly moved, indeed,
By every breath, like to a wind-swept reed.
Already thine own word thou hast forgot;
Thy promise that thou wouldst not leave the spot
Whereon thy servant left thee, till he came.

Florian.

I did, in truth, forget, I own with shame,
Not my word only, but my servant, too!
I must return for him—

FANTASMA.
>Nay, nay, not so!
For he is with the Hermit of the Mill,
And spirits watch, to guard them both from ill.
'Tis better thus. He could not go with thee
Whither I would that thou shouldst follow me,
Thou and the maiden whom thou shalt set free.
Before this time her freedom had been won,
But for Rosemary's fault. Was it well done,
O Fay! impatiently to rush upon
Dangers thou couldst not know? Hadst thou obeyed,
Ere now had been set free this helpless maid.
Weep not! Thou shalt retrieve the fault this night.
>[*Loud Thunder.*

See! the full moon again withdraws her light,
For evil is abroad, and storm-winds come
To drive my fairies to their own bright home.
I cannot long defy the storm-king's power,
For he will sweep in fury through my bower.
Me, he can harm not, but my tender fays
Love moonlit nights, and long, sweet summer-days;
Therefore, I now dismiss my fairy train,
That they may shun the coming flood of rain;
But, thou, my gentle Rosemary, remain.
By thy sweet power and Jack-o'-Lantern's light,
We will aid Florian in his quest to-night.
>[*Thunder. The Fairies vanish.*

Thou, Florian, must retrace the forest wide,

And be the dancing Will-o'-the-Wisp our guide;
And I will teach thee all that must be done,
Ere from her foe the maiden can be won.
Rosemary, come, we walk invisibly.

FLORIAN.

Whither thou wilt, I'll freely follow thee.

[*Exeunt.*

SCENE II. *Before the ruined Church. Storm. Enter* HERMIT *and* DAN.

HERMIT.

Here is the Church. In other, happier days,
True servants of the ONE whom all should praise
Held fitting worship here; now, slaves of sin
With horrid glee, their orgies hold therein;
Like the poor heart, once swept and garnished fair,
Only for demons to inhabit there.
It is a state that pleases Satan well,
Where holiness once dwelt, himself to dwell,
And brows whereon the holy sign has been,
He loves to stamp with his broad seal of sin.

The church windows are illumined from within, and the tones of an organ blend with sounds of revelry. The storm increases.

DAN.

O Sir! What *will* become o' me, dis night?
Less go fum here, or I shell die wid fright!

HERMIT.

What, have you been so brave, to falter now?
Remember, nothing can the truth o'erthrow,
And evil, bravely faced, from goodness flies.
Demons love not to meet an angel's eyes,
Nor strive successfully with prayerful men,
Armed in true meekness.   Let us enter, then,
And, for the event, have neither fear nor care;
For nothing is so strong as faith and prayer.

[*They enter the church.*

SCENE III.   *Interior of the church, brilliantly illuminated. A black Cloud fills the pulpit; an impish Spirit presides at the organ. Wine, etc., on the communion-table, at each side of which stands a beautiful dark Spirit, in flame-colored robes; the one crowned with grapes, and holding a jeweled goblet, the other having a golden crown, and bearing a horn-of plenty.* BEAUCLERC, WITCHES, WIZARDS, *etc.*, LUCIA, *partially unveiled, seated in a chair before the chancel.*

BEAUCLERC.

Now, first of all, join we in that wild chant
To the dread master whom we all adore.

CHANT.

Hail to thee, hail to thee, Spirit of Fire!
  Spirit of Might, whom we dread and adore!

Hail to thee, Chief, whom the nations admire!
Ruler of Earth, in thy pride and thy power!

BEAUCLERC.

And, now, pour out—pour out the wine of youth,
That wrinkled age may drop her withered mask,
And youth herself beam brighter than before!
Drink, and be young! Joy crowns the locks of youth!

The grape-crowned SPIRIT *pours out wine; they crowd to the altar and drink riotously.*

And thou, bright Lucia, needing not this wine
To give thee youth or make thee beautiful,
Yet, drink! For then wilt thou possess a power
The youngest and the fairest cannot wield.

[*She drinks.*

Come, let the organ peal in all its power!
Lucia, arise! I take thee by the hand—

The music stops; the lights grow dim; disorder and confusion.

What now? What mean you? Now the cup is full
And at the lip, why must I lose the draught?

Enter HERMIT *and* DAN.

Lucia, draw close your veil.—What do you here,
Unhappy dotard? Would you seek your death?

HERMIT.

I seek to free the soul thou hast enthralled!

LUCIA.

Where am I? Oh, the dreadful light that breaks
Into the dim recesses of my soul!

BEAUCLERC.

I thought thou hadst been sheltered from all harm,
And from harm-doing, in the arms of sleep.

HERMIT.

Thy spells have failed thee, wizard! Heaven is yet
Too strong to crumble at thy weak command.
Why dost thou stand amazed? Call up thy fiends,
And bid them bear the hermit from thy sight;
Or, speak to these, your instruments and slaves,
And bid them tear the old man limb from limb.
What, pale and silent, still? Then *I* command:
Deliver up to me the stolen maid!

BEAUCLERC.

I shall obey you! Lucia, lift the veil!

LUCIA.

No! I am not the mindless thing I was
Before you gave to me your sorcerer's wine,
And when I heard the voice of this good man
My soul awakened, or returned to me.—
Most reverend father, should I lift this veil,
Whoever looked upon my face would die,
Even he who has enchanted me. Too late—
Too late, I fear, you come to rescue me;
A moment sooner had been well, indeed,
Before I drank the dark magician's wine.
And yet, your coming broke the evil rite;

A moment later, and a mightier spell
Had chained my soul forever.   As it is,
I dare not lift this veil, lest you should die!

      BEAUCLERC, (*to his rabble of witches, etc.*)
Disperse!   Your presence here endangers you,
And helps me not.   Leave me to deal with him.
          [*Witches and Wizards fly confusedly.*

          HERMIT.
Since even *you* dare not behold her face,
Why not restore her to her former state?.
'Tis but a fiend who for the love of sin,
Does wickedness; man sins for fancied gain.
Since you are man, I dare appeal to you,
To reason, to the conscious soul within—
Persist not in this useless wickedness,
Cruel to her and profitless to you.

          BEAUCLERC.
When once the fitting time arrives again
I can complete the spell I have begun.
Meantime, know this: Not even *I* have power
To break the enchantment wherewith she is bound.
To raise that veil, in truth, would snap the charm,
But whosoever lifts the veil must die;
Unless a man could raise it, pure of heart,
And brave as pure, and gentle as courageous.
But where in all the world, is such a man?

Hermit! I claim the maiden as my own!
Let me complete the spell I have begun,
And I restore her to her wonted self.
Old man! I will submit myself to thee,
Will burn my parchments, break my magic rod,
Do anything, be anything you will,
If only you allow my will in this!
So shall you save two souls instead of one.

HERMIT.

Men oft do evil, hoping good will come,
But all such hopes are vain. I will myself
Remove the fatal veil that hides her face.
I am old, and stand already by my grave;
Death has for me no terrors; and far less
If I, in dying, save so bright a life.

BEAUCLERC.

Hold! Hold! We may not take your life, old man!
A stronger Power forbids me (as I wished)
To slay you by the lifting of the veil.

HERMIT.

This is a pretext. I will raise—
A soft clear VOICE *from the cloud.*
Forbear!
[*All stand silent.*

BEAUCLERC, (*in a lower tone*).

Well may you pale! *We* seldom hear that Voice!—
Nor is the gift of your own life, old man,

Sufficient to atone this maiden's sin;
For, know, it was her own sin that betrayed
And placed her as a captive in my power—
The sin of pride in her own purity;
And she forgot to pray before she slept.
We know, as well as saints, the power of prayer!

Lucia.

Alas! I own and I repent my sin,
But yet, good father, I do not despair,
Nor would I take the offered sacrifice,
Your life for mine. It were too high a price;
And I will trust myself to faith and prayer.

Hermit.

But wherefore, if I give my life for hers,
Would not the act suffice to set her free?

Beauclerc.

Snow-pure the man must be who lifts that veil!
Yours is the purity of pardoned sin,
And wisdom you have found in length of years;
You know the emptiness of earthly joys,
For you have proved them all. The approach of death
Would end your penance; and be hailed with joy;
It were no sacrifice for thee to die.
He must be young, who dares to lift that veil,
In the fresh morning of his rosy youth,

When life is rainbow-arched, and doubly dear.
Lucia must pay, too, of her own free will,
Part of her ransom—'tis a costly one!—
Thou brightest Lucia!
Strive not with fate.   If thou, of thy free mind,
Wouldst own allegiance to the Power I serve,
Thou shouldst be queen and dominate the world!

Lucia.

Too oft I've harkened to that voice of thine,
Thou false and cruel as the subtle snake!
Tell me, what is the price that I must pay,
And I will pay it.   I have gifts, thou knowest,
That give me power o'er much of earth; her riches,
Her beauty, or what else thou most desirest;
Her gentler spirits will yield all to thee.

Voice *from the cloud.*

That which is hardest for thee to give,
What costs thee most to yield, will I receive.

Lucia.

I will pile the red gold, a glittering heap,
    On the sacred altar stone;
I will seek the pure pearl from the watery deep,
Bright gems from the vale where the hot winds sleep—
    Will these for my sin atone?

VOICE.

Not this—not this will pay the price,
All the riches of earth in sacrifice.

LUCIA.

I will gather the lovliest flowers of spring
    That fairy bowers display;
I will seek them at dawn, ere the rude winds fling
The dew from their opening cups. I will bring
The sweetest and best of each blossoming thing,
    Vine-wreath or flowery spray!

VOICE.

Not this! Not this! 'Twill not suffice,
All the beauty of earth in sacrifice.

LUCIA.

Rich music, in one melting strain
    Shall all sweet sounds combine,
From the foaming cataract's wild refrain,
To the tinkling bells of the silver rain—
From the breeze that sighs through rustling cane
And lisping reeds that sigh again,
    To the wind-harp in the pine!

VOICE.

Not this—not this will pay the price
    That sets the captive free;

Though thou bring all the wealth in earth that lies,
All the beauty of new-found Paradise,
And mingle the music of earth and of skies,
Not music, nor beauty, nor wealth would suffice
    To lift that veil for thee!

          HERMIT.

Despair not yet, sweet maid! Nor deem one sin,
The single flaw within a priceless gem,
Will render thee the thrall of this dark Power.
Give up all pride; *that* is the sacrifice!
And, meekly bending to the will of heaven,
Now and forever learn the strength of patience;
Patient endurance is the crown of strength!

          BEAUCLERC.

Hermit, this night is ours! Though thou hast stood,
With courage I could almost reverence,
In the dark shadow of Tremendous Might,
Yet, yield to destiny! Thine hour is past,
And ours, full-armed in strength, is here. Old man,
I would not injure thee; thou art my foe,
As all the slaves of heaven; yet, brave of heart,
I would not touch thee roughly. Yield thou must,
Nor look upon our sacred mysteries.
Sleep, thou, in trance; unharmed, unharming.

        VOICE (*soft and low*).
        Sleep!

HERMIT.

I will not sleep! My brain—mine eyes are heavy,
Yet I will still resist—my senses reel—

The HERMIT *sinks down in a trance;* SPIRITS *rise with him and disappear.*

BEAUCLERC.

Yet there is one within this wood to-night
Whom I fear most of all; the beardless youth;
Before him I still tremble and shrink back,
As he had some strange power that conquers mine.

FIRST SPIRIT.

Wait, thou, in silence! Lo, the Ruling One
Takes thy veiled captive in the awful cloud.

LUCIA.

O help me—save! The trial is too sharp!

The Cloud envelopes LUCIA, *and immediately disappears.*

SECOND SPIRIT.

The maid—a prize worth all the toil of capture
To thee and us—may yet be lost to thee,
And to our Master, through a fault of thine.
Thou didst far underrate Fantasma's power,
And thou didst shrink, weakly, from thought of harming
This boy, who is to Lucia's heart so dear.
One way remains: Try all thy power to tempt,
Aided by us, young Florian. Snare his soul,
And share with him thy earthly power and glory.

FIRST SPIRIT.
If our enticements fail with Florian,
Lucia is lost to us.

BEAUCLERC.
No! If we fail,
Fantasma shall complete what we begin,
And aid our purpose in her own despite!
Our Master has his time of power with her,
As with all things of earth, however pure;
And she already trembles at the thought
Of possible harm befalling Florian;
For she has loved the poet from his youth,
And, when I sought her, fled from me to him.

FIRST SPIRIT.
He comes! And shielded by Fantasma's power.
Deal thou with him, and we will cope with her,
Fairest and strongest of the earth-born powers.
Enter FLORIAN, FANTASMA *and* ROSEMARY.

SECOND SPIRIT.
Fair sister, welcome!

FIRST SPIRIT.
We have waited long.

FANTASMA.
Ye call me sister? *Ye*, unknowing ought
Of kindred or of love? Demons ye are,

As loveless as your elemental fires,
And hideous as the chaos whence ye sprung,
Though shining now in shapes of borrowed beauty.

First Spirit.

Whatever we may be, thou knowest well
Our power, which now we choose to set apart,
O bright-browed phantom! to confer with thee.

Second Spirit.

The maid thou seekest is not now with us;
But we will freely tell, and show thee, too,
Where she now is, and how she may be won.
Being thyself a spirit, thou shouldst know
It sometimes suits a demon to speak truth
For his own purpose. Harken thou to us!

Fantasma slowly approaches; they confer apart.

Florian.

Why dost thou smile on me, with open brow?
There can be only strife between us two.

Beauclerc.

Nay, Florian! We both erred—and I the most,
Being elder, and, it may be, better versed
In things it much imports us both to know;
We erred, I say, in choosing enmity
When friendship better aids our purposes,
Both thine and mine. Thou art beneath a spell,

Seeking, thou neither knowest whom nor what,
Because thy queen Fantasma wills it so.
She whom thou seekest, thou shalt find this night;
Nay, I myself will lead thee to her presence,
If thou wilt call me friend and clasp my hand.

FLORIAN.

Sooner than clasp thy hand, incarnate falsehood!
I would—

BEAUCLERC.

   Strike off thine own clean hand, no doubt!
But spare invective, useless as discourteous.
Thinkest thou the darkness better loves the light
Than light loves darkness? Never think it, Florian!
I am thy natural foe, as thou art mine;
Thy presence is not soothing to my soul!
Yet I seek peace, and give thee courteous words.
The angels do not rail upon the demons;
Though thou may'st teach the angels purity,
A sorcerer yet excels thee in good manners.

FLORIAN.

Thy taunt is just. I will not rail on thee,
But hear with patience all thou hast to say;
Only, bear this in mind :—Or soon, or late,
The maid thou hast enthralled will I set free.

BEAUCLERC.

But how, if I should yield her to thy hand?

FLORIAN.
And wilt thou?

BEAUCLERC.
On conditions.

FLORIAN.
Ah! I thought
There was some deeper purpose. We waste time!

BEAUCLERC.
You promised to hear all I had to say.

FLORIAN.
Speak, then, but briefly; for my patience wears.

BEAUCLERC.
I love this maiden as *thou* canst not love;
Thou who art all unconscious of her name.
Speak not! I know the fairy-queen's commands
That thou pursue this quest for virtue merely,
With faith and patience, seeking not to know
For whom thou laborest, till success is thine;
But, hear me! All my spirit knows of love,
And all it hopes of happiness or peace,
Is wound about this girl. I love her, Florian!
I seek her not because she brings me power—
At least, not *all* for that. Her slender hand
Holds the fine, golden chain that links my soul
To its last hope of virtue : snap that chain,
You break my last, frail, trembling hold on heaven!

But what is this to thee, who knowest not sin,
Nor its unfailing shadow, wretchedness?
He only who has sinned can pity sin;
But *thou* art white as snow, and far more cold.

FLORIAN.

Who has not sinned of Adam's ruined race?
I have not fallen by mine own act so low
As thou, because I have been fenced from ill.
Think'st thou I deem myself thy better? No!
Thou mayest re-trim the lamp of thy strong soul,
Whose powerful light would dull my feeble ray.

BEAUCLERC.

Kind are thy words, and I would fain believe
Thy soul as kind. Do not reject my prayer!
I would repent—but ah! thou dost not know
How bitter is the herb that's called repentance!
Like a sick, froward child, the soul rejects
The unpalatable medicine. One hope
Is mine, and only one: it lies in her,
The captive maid, for whom we are at strife.
What is it you fear for her? Would I bring harm
On her I worship? The least ring of hair
That lies like light upon her innocent brow,
Is more to me than—wherefore do I speak,
Baring my soul before unfriendly eyes?
I have sinned; I suffer; better fate be thine,
Who still art young, and pure as once I was.

FANTASMA.

FLORIAN.
Indeed, with all my soul I pity thee!

BEAUCLERC.
Behold! the fairy queen has ceased to speak
With her less favored sisters; such they are,
Although rejected by Fantasma's pride.

FANTASMA.
Florian! The trial is before thee now;
I may not, and I cannot, aid thee more.
The conflict of a soul is all its own.
Yet, I can warn thee: oh, be strong and brave,
Watchful and prayerful! all depends on thee.
I now depart to seek the captive maid,
To see with mine own eyes if true or false
Is the unwelcome tale these spirits tell.
I will return with speed: remain thou here,
Till my return. I leave thee not unguarded,
Though in the conflict thou must be alone.
[*She vanishes.*

BEAUCLERC.
The bright-browed fairy-queen is cold and pure,
Pitiless as some human souls have been,
In the clear diamond of whose purity
There are no flaws of tenderness; but see,
These spirits, dark, indeed, yet beautiful,
And with such gentleness of lip and brow!
These are no demons, Florian!

FLORIAN.
                    What are they?
They cannot be good angels, though their beauty
Is more than mortal; dark and starry eyes
That seem so full of tenderness! they smile,
But sorrow looks from those dark, liquid depths.
What are they?

BEAUCLERC.
            Merely shadows of earth's beauty,
Fantasma's sisters, though she owns them not,
Because she dwells in light, and they in shade.—
Florian, wert thou my friend, and wouldst consent
That I espouse this maiden—earth sees not
Nor ever saw, the monarch thou shouldst be;
Such sovereignty, such splendor, such renown,
Not Solomon the matchless ever knew!

FLORIAN.
Why dost thou proffer me such splendid gifts,
Thyself remaining poor and all unknown?

BEAUCLERC.
Riches are mine, would I put forth my hand;
But, heretofore, I have sinned royally,
Which he can never do, who sins for gain.
I have not cared for gold. Thou doubtest this?
Behold, the senseless idol of the world!

The gold-crowned Spirit shakes from her Cornucopia a shower of gold and gems.

First Spirit.

Yes! Thou shalt be king, if thou hast but the will,
   And gifted more richly than Midas of old.
The spirit of fortune shall wait on thee still,
Thy roses shall diamonds for dew-drops distill,
   And the sand in thy foot-print shall glitter with gold!

Florian.

Have I, then, shown so poor and mean a mind,
You tempt me with the riches you despise?
I know that life has better gifts than gold.

Beauclerc.

Yet is unbounded wealth a kingly gift.

Florian.

I ask not this, nor any gift, of thee.

Beauclerc.

True; but I still may proffer; thou refuse,
Or take, as pleases thee. Life holds, indeed,
Gifts better, far, than gold; the chief of which
Is something often sought, but never found,
Or lost as soon as found—immortal youth!

Florian.

I as no other immortality
Than that which heaven bestows on every man.

FANTASMA.

BEAUCLERC.

But see! Arcania pours for thee the wine
That warmed heroic hearts of olden time,
And mingled subtly with the circling blood,
Till they became as gods, strong to endure
And to enjoy, the evil and the good;
Splendid in fadeless, beautiful, bright youth,
Their lives on-stretching through such length of days
As makes an earthly immortality.
Look on the sparkling liquid as it flows!
Now, a translucent stream of ruddy gold;
Again, it gives a crimson glow, like blood
Restless with the quick principle of life;
Gleaming with changing hues and rainbow lights,
Like a clear lake beneath a sunset sky.
Florian!
There's not the smallest bubble shining there
In opal beauty, but contains some gift
Of strength or glory more than monarchs know.
Drink! And thy veins receive undying youth,
And health, and beauty! But these are not much.
Drink! And thy mind shall bask in heavenly light,
Thy soul shall float on tideless seas of bliss,
And all thy dreams be sweet realities.
This, also, is not much; the hopes of youth,
Though realized, are little worth. But drink!
And thou shalt reign supreme o'er thine own self,
That triple self of body, mind and soul;

Life's pangs and fears shall crouch like lions tamed;
Her pleasures strew thy conquering way with flowers;
And thou, whose frank and tender heart now bleeds
At every coarse or cruel touch, shalt stand
In thine own calm and self-sufficing strength,
And in thy soul-serenity, a god!

FLORIAN.

Thou think'st to tempt me, and dost but arouse
My pity for thyself, unhappy man!
Dost thou believe all happiness must lie
In sovereignty? I envy not that man
Who thinks it degradation to obey;
Obedience is the soul's necessity.
Whatever we love deeply, that we place
Far, far above ourselves. The soul's delight
Is, to forget or sacrifice to love
All thoughts of self; it is the lover's bliss
To throne his lady and to worship her;
Friend worships friend with self-regardless love;
And ah! what bliss is theirs who kneel to heaven
In the obedience born of trusting love!
This, thou hast never known. In thy mad search
After a non-existent liberty,
Thou gladly wouldst dethrone the King of Heaven.
And *thou* wouldst reign? Wouldst be a god? Supreme
Must be the love of self in thy dark soul!

BEAUCLERC.

I've wasted time in parley with a slave
Who hugs his chain and worships him who smites.
May'st thou with cords of steel be lashed to death,
Thou servile foe of light and liberty!

Re-enter FANTASMA.

FLORIAN.

Never wert thou so welcome! Let us go,
I pray thee, from this desecrated place;
And thou wilt guide me to this hapless maid.

FANTASMA.

Yes, come! This is no place for thee or me.

BEAUCLERC.

Nay, Virtue most superlative! Fly not.
Ye have disordered and dispersed our circle,
And so we leave to Virtue's cleansing power
The meeting-place you grudge to us. Adieu,
Until we meet again, when *ye* shall fly! [*Exit.*
Spirits vanish, with mocking laughter, which is echoed by invisible beings filling the Church.

FLORIAN.

O horrible! The air is full of evil!
Fantasma, let us go—but, who is this,
Lying in trance or slumber so profound?
It is my servant, Dan! Harmless and kind,

And helpless in his ignorance, they have not—
Surely, they have not injured him?

FANTASMA.

     Fear not!
'Tis but a trancèd slumber that enfolds him;
Rosemary shall awake and guide him hence.
But, Florian, do not call him ignorant!
Wisdom lies oftener in the heart than head,
And Dan has done more for the captive maid
Than either you or I; he brought the Hermit
Before the binding spell was made complete.
 We came too late! Had you but sought my bower
When first you met Rosemary, we had saved
The helpless and imprisoned one; but now—

FLORIAN.

Ah, fairy-queen, say not, *it is too late!*
Nothing can be too late that heaven approves.

FANTASMA.

'Tis true, and yet—. Come, then; thou shalt know all!
Rosemary, take the servant to your care,
And bear him to the Hermit of the Mill,
Whom those dark spirits did not dare to harm:
They merely bore him to his hermitage,
Sleeping a pleasant sleep beneath a spell.

FLORIAN.

And will poor Dan be safe?

FANTASMA.
      As infancy
Beneath the mother's eye. Have thou no fear!
From this hour till the dawn, my subjects rule
This haunted grove, and drive the witches hence.
Rosemary, awake and guard him with due care!
Come, Florian! there is much for *thee* to hear!
    [*Exeunt* FANTASMA *and* FLORIAN.

ROSEMARY.
Rise, thou, who in thy ignorance art wise,
And strong in weakness. I will lead thee hence
To safety; and this night shalt thou know joy
Such as thy dumb soul never felt before.
Nay, do not speak! This wand upon thy lips
Insures thy silence. Let us leave this place!
        [*Exeunt.*

SCENE IV. *The Fairy Glen.*

Enter FANTASMA *and* FLORIAN.

FANTASMA.
Thou shalt know all.
    There is a gloomy cave
Deep hidden in the center of the earth,
Controlled by spirits evil past all thought—
A cave that never knew the light of day,
Nor heard the echo of a human voice.

Within this dreadful place, the captive maid
Is held, still shrouded in the fatal veil,
And doubly shrouded in a cloud of darkness.
I may not tell thee what that cloud contains!
Enough, that, if thou rashly enterest there
Thou diest—unless unshaken courage be
Thy sword, and spotless purity thy shield.
Speak—hast thou courage such as martyrs know,
And is thy soul pure as an angel's prayer?

FLORIAN.

I think, to save another I could die;
For purity, no soul is free of sin.
I dare not venture in my own poor strength;
My weapons must be courage, faith and prayer.

FANTASMA.

Thou knowest not the dreadful power of Sin;
Thou knowest not with whom thy soul must strive!

FLORIAN.

What will betide the maiden if I fail?

FANTASMA.

If thou once raise that veil, though *thou* shouldst die,
The maid is free, and safe forevermore.

FLORIAN.

Then I will venture! O may I but live

To lift that veil and set the captive free;
Though in the self-same moment I should die!

FANTASMA.

Yet stay! There's time enough—and though thou
    wearest
Thy life so lightly, it is dear to me!
And, having shown thee what thou hast to fear,
Thou shalt behold a part of all thou losest
By throwing life away in this wild quest.

A magic sea lies hidden in this wood,
    Invisible to dull and earthly sight:
On that sweet shore no mortal ever stood,
    Nor cast a shadow on those waves of light.

The souls of those I love have wandered there,
    Flying from sordid care, or grief, or shame;
But gross mortality in that fine air
    Would perish, as at touch of burning flame.

And, on the bosom of that fairy sea,
    An island of unfading beauty lies;
There the enamored winds move languidly
    O'er blooming orange-groves and bowers of spice;

And gorgeous wreaths of crimson-blossomed vines
    Go winding through the aromatic woods:
The golden jasmine and the grape entwines,
    And rich pomegranates blushing red as blood.

And everywhere, amid the fragrant green
   Of orange-groves,—by every sweet lagoon,
In soft mimosa-shaded vales, are seen
   Fairy pavilions, glittering in the moon.

There, life and music flow, so sweetly blending,
   Time falls asleep among the passion-flowers:
With circling grace, in dances never-ending,
   On silver sandals move the enchanted hours.

The moon is larger there, the stars more tender,
   For on this isle the sunlight never beams:—
Thou shalt behold this land in all its splendor,
   Which other eyes have only seen in dreams!

The Cliff opens, in the background, and the Fairy Sea appears:
Fairy Isles in the distance.

FLORIAN.

Enchanting scene! O isles divinely fair!
The soul of beauty must in truth lie there!
Such must the unsullied Eden-isles have been,
Before the shadow fell of death or sin.
Would that I might forever dwell with thee
In those fair isles beyond that smiling sea!

FANTASMA.

   Then come, beloved, with me!
In yon soft isles, where shining palaces
Gleam through green groves of golden-fruited trees,
Where the light winds the blossomed roses shake,

And white star-jessamine, until they make
A summer snow-storm, drifting flake by flake
  Over the perfumed grasses of the lea;
  There, oh! there awaiteth thee
More bliss than thou canst take!

   FLORIAN.

And shall I, then, forsake this hapless maid,
For whom at first thou didst bespeak my aid?
  And she must perish there,
If I forsake her now, in the dark shade
  Of danger and despair.

   FANTASMA.

Should *I* not save her, if she could be saved?
  Already, I have braved
Dangers thou knowest not; and shall I see
Thee, also, perish? Nay, it must not be!
Cast the sad memory from thy pensive mind.—
  Behold, the fairy kind,
Summoned to meet thee here, are gaily springing
From field and forest; hear their silver singing!
*Sweet sounds of rustling leaves, chirping birds, and rippling
  water. The* WOOD-SPIRITS *appear.*

   FLORIAN.

O beautiful! O wondrous! What are these
That drop like falling nuts from shaken trees,
Or like the painted leaves that Autumn showers

To make amends for the lost summer flowers!
Most small and dainty figures, light of wing,
From tree, and shrub, and tufted grass they spring!
And not a flower so small but there doth dwell
A tiny fay to guard its fragrant cell!
And other, larger forms—how bright they come,
Emerging from the green wood's bowery gloom;
Taller are they; more human; more like *thee!*
With many-colored garments, tresses free,
And garlanded with flowers of richest dyes;
Winged, some like birds, and some like butterflies;
Some crowned with laurel and with ivy-shoots,
And nodding heads of wheat; some bearing fruits,
And others, still, with fine and fairy flutes,
Fashioned from reeds and stalks of hollow cane.
But, hark, how sweetly sing the blooming train!

SONG OF THE WOOD-SPIRITS.
O come to us, our poet and our king!
  We are the spirits of the fields and woods;
  All sunny heights, all shady solitudes,
Are ours, and ours the pleasures they may bring.

Are not the spirits of the woodlands fair?
Look on the clustering curls of our rich hair!
  All lovely tints are there,
From corn-silk brightness to black-purple luster
Of wreathing wild-grape's shadow-ripened cluster;
From the green moss that lines a woodland spring,

To the grey mosses from live-oaks that swing;
    From the soft waving of the maiden-hair
To the sweet fringe-tree's snowy tasseling!
    Are we not very fair?
        [*Echo. Very fair.*

We vary in our shape as in our size;
    Look in our smiling eyes!
    There each soft color lies,
Of fruit or floweret, from the brilliant blue
Of the wild iris to the violet's hue;
From chestnut and the brown cone of the pine
To jetty chinquapin or muscadine!

    Are we not very fair?
        The eglantine
Has left her courtship with the air;
Has left the coral woodbine's clasping twine,
And on our tender cheeks, more waxen-fair
Than the rich petals of magnolias are,
    She spreads a bloom that owes
Its pale perfection to the sweet wild rose.
        [*Echo. The sweet wild rose!*

    Yet, merely types are we,
    Though beautiful we be,
Of beauty and of bliss awaiting thee!
        [*Echo. Awaiting thee!*

FLORIAN.

On wings like humming-bird in sunlight glancing;
On airy feet, retreating and advancing;
Gliding, circling, from the earth up-springing;
Wheeling, floating, from vine-garlands swinging;
Lightly embracing, airily chasing,
With linked hands in circles interlacing!
Echo prolongs the sounds entrancing,
Till all the woody glades are filled with music and with dancing!

[*The* WOOD-FAIRIES *vanish. Low, mellow thunder; the* FIRE-SPRITES *appear, with flashes of light preceding them.*]

FLORIAN.

Ah! What are those bright shapes that shining glide
From yonder cavern in the mountain-side?
More bright, but not more lovely than the fays
Of field and forest, are these forms of grace,
Clad royally in robes of spangling gold
And twinkling silver, every gleaming fold
Crusted with richest jewels of the mine.
On those bright brows what starry diamonds shine!
And rainbow-tinted fires, in lambent play,
Curl round the auburn locks that wildly stray,
And dark, resplendent eyes make pale the glow
Of flames and jewels shining round them so!

FIRE-SPRITES.

We dwell in central fires and hidden caves;
    Earth's treasures all are ours;
Her forces are our captives and our slaves,
    And we direct her powers.

To thee shall open every dark recess;
    Thou shalt our strength employ
On whom thou wilt, to blight them or to bless,
    To make, or to destroy.

[*The* FIRE-SPRITES *vanish. A sound of Eolian Harps; the* CLOUD-FAYS *descend.*]

FLORIAN.

Yet more, and brighter! Like a shower of stars,
Or Eden-birds escaped the golden bars,
The bright-haired spirits of the clouds and sky,
Borne upon starry wings, go flashing by!
Robed as in clouds of silvery, snowy white,
Or veiled in melting azure, starry-bright
With lights that come and go; while changing sheen
Of tender rose and orange tints are seen!
Floating above each head, a sparkling tiar
Hangs like a hazy ring of silver fire,
Wherein bright sparkles come and go, now kindle, now expire!

THE SYLPHS.

We the bright spirits are
Of fleecy clouds and azure skies,

Steeped in the sunset's gorgeous dyes;
    And in our luminous eyes
We hold the sweetness of the evening star—
Of all clear stars, whose tender sheen
    Is pensive and serene.

And yet, we are not given to sadness wholly;
We dwell not in the dreaming cloudland solely;
We have the splendid smiles of dying day;
We have the young moon's most bewitching ray;
        And unto us is given
    The happy light that beams
    Into a poet's dreams,
And the still joy that draws the soul to heaven.

    Ah, Poet, we can yield
    More bliss than wood or field,
    Or jeweled cave, or central fires,
    To the soul whose pure desires
    Are such as thine must be;
    Not even the powerful sea
Can give those joys serene and high which we may promise thee.

[*The* CLOUD FAYS *melt into a silvery mist, and vanish. The sound of billows:* WATER-NYMPHS *and* SIRENS *arise from the Sea.*]

        FLORIAN.
Behold, where, rising from the fairy lake
And still lagoon, whose smoothèd waters break

In dimpling eddies and in circles wide,
The water-maidens come in all their pride!
The bending lilies kiss those forms that bless
The clinging wave with their white loveliness;
Far-flowing locks of crinkling hair, that toss
In wavy length, like tangled river-moss,
Veil shining shoulders, and the snowy charms
Of glistening bosoms and of rounded arms,
While from the showery tresses lightly fall
Pearl-shining drops, with tinklings musical.
Sea-weed, and pearl, and coral's branching stem,
Prismatic shells, and many an ocean gem,
Entwined with flowing sprays of rosemary,
Crown them with wreaths that shine so radiantly,
They cast on rippling lake and smooth lagoon
Circles of light, like haloes round the moon.
But, richer than all gems, their star-like eyes
Shine with a siren's subtle witcheries,
Changeful as hues of ocean, and as bright;
Now, soft and deeply blue as lazulite;
Now, sparkling with full joy, and crystalline
As the green glitter of aqua marine.
O lucent brows! O cheeks whose delicate flush
Is clearer than the sea-shell's finest blush!
O full, sweet lips! whence flows the song that swells
Above the harps, above the silver shells!

What need have ye of harp or shell?   Those liquid tones
   express
Music's full soul, a world of love, and worlds of happiness!

The Sea-Nymphs.
We pledge thee faith, we hail thee king!
For thee our golden harps shall ring,
For thee our sweetest songs we sing—
                        For thee, for only thee!
Our shining halls are gay for thee;
Our fairy barque shall stay for thee;
We smooth the star-lit way for thee,
                        Across the sparkling sea!

[*The* MERMAIDENS *disappear.   A fairy Boat floats across the
        Sea toward* FLORIAN.]

Florian.
O too much hast thou shown me!   Tempt no more
My troubled heart!   If *thou* hast not the power
To move me, can *these* have, though fair they be?
Fairer and brighter than aught else but thee!
And when wert thou so beautiful as now?
A soft, sweet radiance lights that lovely brow;
Thy hair—how shall its brightness be expressed?
The golden flame that lights an oriole's breast;
Ripe wheat, tipped goldenly by sunset's ray; ·
Or clustering fireflies on a drooping spray!
And what is like the beauty of thine eyes?
The clear-green crystal of a spring that lies

Deep in a wood and bowered in thick vines
Of glossy ivy and smooth muscadines;
The light of emeralds; or the green-rayed star
Of earth herself, shining to worlds afar!
Fairer by far than even that beauteous band,
Thy subject-fays, who people Fairyland,
And more bewitching than the varying sheen
Of thy bright wand, whose splendors opaline
Are drawn from earth, and air, and sky, and sea,
Blending all spells of subtlest witchery!

FANTASMA.

If I, indeed, am beautiful to thee,
    Come thou with me!
    Thou canst not know
What bliss, what beauty, what full ecstasy,
    I can bestow!
All I have shown thee of beauty and power
Is merely the show of a vanishing hour,
    A type, and no more!
But glory shall weave thee a garland divine,
Beauty unveiled in her splendor shall shine,
Pleasure, and power, and fame shall be thine—
    If thou wilt be mine!
The spirit of music shall bow to thy will
Till thy bosom is calm, and thy pulses are still;
The inmost recess of thy soul it shall fill,
    Till thou lose the remembrance of wrong!
All day shall the low, liquid sound of a rill

Be blent with the oriole's tremulous trill,
All night the swift, silver-winged moments shall thrill
    To the mocking-bird's passion of song!

There shall the asphodel brighten thy bower,
    Rich with the odors of blossoming pine;
The amaranth bloom by the sweet passion flower,
    Emblems of faith and of beauty divine:
There is the life for which nature has meant thee;
There shalt thou drink of the poet's nepenthe;
Heaven-sent food of the soul shall content thee—
    Earth in her beauty and glory be thine!

FLORIAN.

Spirit of loveliness! From that first hour
When I beheld thee, I confessed thy power:
Whatever sweet disguise thou didst assume
Of winter's dazzle or of summer's bloom,
Shining in orbéd lights from starry skies,
Or brightening earth with gleams of Paradise;
Or if, in lighter mood, wouldst dance away
The hours with frolic fauns, as wild as they;
Ever I yielded to thy soft control;
But *now*—shall I with falsehood stain my soul,
And cruelty? Shall I my forehead brand
With cowardice? No! Not for Fairyland!
Look not upon me thus! It may not be
That I yield now to thy sweet witchery:
I will not sin for Fairyland—or thee!

FANTASMA.

O keep that soul forever bright and clear!
Ah, Florian, never wert thou half so dear;
Never so worthy love, as now thou art!
I will to Fairyland at once depart,
And send thee thence whatever help I may.
To the dark cavern take thy lonely way,
And meet the terrors that await thee there
With heavenly armor—courage, faith and prayer.

She enters the fairy Boat. As FLORIAN *watches it glide away to Fairyland, the scene closes.*

PART IV.

SCENE I. *A great Cavern far underground, lighted by a weird twilight from the inner recesses. In the center, a thick Cloud. Muttered Thunder.*

Enter FLORIAN; *sharp Lightning and a peal of Thunder, echoed through the inner caverns.*

FLORIAN.
Whatever living thing is in this cave,
I charge you, by the Name that most you fear,
A Name that cannnot lightly leave the lip—
Give me your aid to save the soul I seek!
 [*Thunder; vivid lightning leaps from the Cloud.*
If thou art good, O dweller in the Cloud!
I charge thee, in the name of Supreme Goodness,
The name of—
[*Crashing Thunder drowns the voice of* FLORIAN, *and is repeated through remote windings of the Cave.*]
Lend me thine aid! If evil, I command thee,
By the same powerful name—give up thy prey!
 [*The roar of a mighty Wind shakes the Cavern.*]

VOICE *from the Cloud.*

Depart!

FLORIAN.

Release the captive, and I go,
Nor seek to unveil thy dreadful mysteries,
Abhorrent to all goodness as to light.

VOICE *from the Cloud.*

What seekest thou?

FLORIAN.

           I know but this—a captive;
A veiled maiden, innocent and pure;
The child of heaven, though now within thy power.

[*A low and sweet but mocking laugh rings through the Cavern in soft musical echoes. The pallid light slowly dies away. Darkness and Silence.* FLORIAN *still remains as at his entrance. Then the Cloud glows with faint light, deepening slowly to intense flame; the lurid Cloud takes the indistinct shape of a giant Demon, and moves toward* FLORIAN.]

FLORIAN.

I fear thee not, thou most appalling Shape,
Although I cannot look on thee unmoved!
By this most holy cross, I bid thee stay!
By all its shadows forth, I bid thee yield,
And render now to me the captive maid!

[*Long, rolling Thunder; the Cloud arises and disappears,* LUCIA *is seen, veiled, in the Center of the Cave, which is again lighted by the dim twilight.*]

'Tis she! It but remains to lift that veil,
And she is safe! Yes, I, indeed, may perish,
But she will go in freedom from this place;
Ay, free as air, and white as purity!—
I will put every thought of self away,
And venture, trusting the o'er-ruling Good;
And, should I die, at least I have not failed,
Because another life is bought with mine.

He advances to LUCIA *and raises the veil. A burst of triumphant music from the interior.*

LUCIA.

My brother! my dear brother!

FLORIAN.

      Can it be
My Lucia! My one sister, my twin-soul!
  BEUCLERC *rushes in, with a drawn saber.*

BEAUCLERC.

Not yet—not yet thy triumph is complete!
Though thou hast conquered Darkness and despair,
I'll vanquish thee, in spite of hell or heaven!
 [*He attacks* FLORIAN : *the sword breaks in pieces.*]
I will not yield! Power yet remains to me!—
Inferior demons, ye who loathe the light,
Ye who exist to hate and to destroy!
Rise to my bidding—rise, and seize, and slay!

[*Shadowy Forms appear, thronging from the interior of the Cavern: they press toward the Brother and Sister, and continue to grow more distinct and menacing.*]

LUCIA.

Alas! my brother, must thou die for me?

FLORIAN.

Nay, do not fear, my sister! Thou art saved!
[*The* FIRE-SPIRITS *appear: soft light fills the Cavern, which glitters like a crystal Grotto. The* FIRE-KING *describes, with his wand, a circle round* LUCIA *and* FLORIAN, *inclosing them in a ring of white fire. The Demons pause.*]

BEAUCLERC.

Eternal cowards! Draw ye back for this?
Ye, who are formed of never-dying flame?
Seize them, and slay!

THE VOICE.

     Depart! the hour is past.
[*The Demons disappear.* BEAUCLERC, *rushing toward* FLORIAN, *the* FIRE-KING *touches the Magician's breast with his burning wand:* BEAUCLERC *falls senseless.*]

THE FIRE-KING.

Wiser is he, who (like a child pursuing
 A firefly), takes delight in simple things,
Than he who follows, to his own undoing,
 The perilous path to Nature's hidden springs;

The fool of science, to his bosom wooing
   A flame that bears destruction on its wings!

(*To Florian:*)
   Hail! victor, who hast driven from our home
     The cloud that on it lay!
   The gentle fairy of the mine, the gnome,
   The fire-sprite, all, to welcome thee have come,—
     To honor thee, who drove the cloud away!

Receive this gift—this little crystal sphere,
   Hollow within, to hold a golden light;
A charmed fairy lamp, whose rays appear
   Through the surrounding crystal, starry-bright.
I place it like a jewel on thy breast:
   O guard with jealous care the starry spark!
Let none this fairy favor from thee wrest,
   Nor ever let the crystal sphere grow dark.

Bright Lucia, free forever from the veil!
   Bind thrice about thy waist this jeweled zone,
This slender snake, whose every golden scale
   Is rich with lucid pearl or precious stone.

THE FIRE-SPRITES.

The mystic veil is gone
   That hath hid so long thy face,
And the silver light of dawn
   Fills this cold and gloomy place;
And the sweet and subtle grace

Of that light so long withdrawn
   Spreads its tender beams apace
   Through the dim and breathless space:
For the interposing veil is rent and gone!

And we, the guardian powers
   Of the central earth, in state
Will bear thee to the bowers
   Where the woodland spirits wait
   For thy coming, all elate
With a greater joy than ours;
All the spirits of the flowers,
Of the mountain, of the wood,
Of the field, and of the flood,

With wingéd motion fleet
   Will haste to welcome thee,
Kneeling gladly at thy feet,
   And at his who set thee free!
      The Scene Closes.

SCENE II. *The Fairy Glen.* ROSEMARY, BROWNIES *and* FAUNS.

        ROSEMARY.
Where have you left your simple-hearted guest,
The servant Dan, committed to your care?

        HAZEL (*a faun*).
He sleeps in my green covert in the woods.

REDBUD (*a browny*).

We charmed him, that he should not yet awake,
And gave him dreams, the sweetest that may be. —
But, Rosemary, 'tis long we've waited here,
Yet Lucia comes not, nor young Florian.

[*Glad music, underground. Auroral lights play in the Sky.*]

ROSEMARY.

She comes! She comes! The dark horizon shows
Auroral lines of amethyst and rose,
    And silver-purple shootings!
Welcome to her who makes the moonlight pale!
Welcome to him whose true heart did not fail!
The flying echoes all along the vale
    Take up our fairy flutings,
In tender tones that rise, and fade and fail,
        The victor hail!

[*Echoes. Hail! Hail!*

[*Subterranean music. A founiatn of golden flame bursts from the earth, then changes to a circle of rainbow fires. The Fire-King appears with* LUCIA *and* FLORIAN *in the midst of the Ring.*]

FIRE-KING.

Sing welcome to the beautiful and brave;
  Weave them fresh chaplets of your fairest flowers,
And call the spirits of the cloud and wave
  To guide them to Fantasma's fairy bowers.

Our pleasing part of this sweet task is done :
'Tis yours to finish what we have begun.
[*The* Fire King *descends and the Circle of Flame disappears.*]

FLORIAN.

Beautiful spirits! Ere you lead us hence
To Fairyland, may we not see the Hermit
And my poor servant? Loving and true-hearted
Is he, although a slave; and dear to me.
May he not go with us to Fairyland?

ROSEMARY.

Whatever he has power to do may be.
Behold, they come, the Hermit and your servant,
And you shall judge if either has the power
To follow you into Fantasma's land.

Enter Hermit *and* DAN, *led by the Wood Spirits.* LUCIA *and* FLORIAN *kneel to the* Hermit.

HERMIT.

Arise, my children, gentle, brave and true!
Much have ye dared, and much have overcome;
But ye must leave this haunted wood in haste,
Nor view the wonders of the Fairyland.
Beauteous is the show of this vain world,
 Yet "beautiful" means hidden evil merely;
Which your untutored hearts have long adored.

ROSEMARY.

Old man, art thou so ancient, wise, and good,
And yet so blindly ignorant? In truth,
There is a lesson set for thee to learn.—
Ye spirits of the flowerland, Oriole
And Mariposa, lead the Hermit hence
To meet Fantasma in her moonlit isles.—
Fear not, old man! We touch with reverent hands
Thy silver locks, enriched by costly time:
To age, not less than virtue, do we bow.
Fear not to go with us! Too little known
Are we to thee, dear as thou art to us.
Go! and this lovely pair shall meet thee soon
In fair Fantasma's pleasure-laden bowers.

[*Fairies lead off the* Hermit, *whom* ROSEMARY *touches with her wand.*]

FLORIAN.

But, why, since we shall meet in Fairyland,
May we not altogether journey thither?

ROSEMARY.

The good old Hermit cannot follow you;
Your starry path lies high above the clouds,
But he, though always looking to the skies,
Must keep the solid earth beneath his feet.
As for your servant, (quicker far than you
To see with superstition's double sight,)
The fine, ethereal forms that wait on you

He cannot see, nor touch, nor understand.
Try him! He knows me, a half-human sprite;
He can discern the glancing Will-o'-the-Wisp;
He knows, and fears, a demon or a witch;
But point him to these thin, aërial shapes:
Bid him look on the fairy Eglantine.

Florian.

Come hither, Dan, and look not thus amazed.
Since last we parted, whither have you been?

Dan.

All 'bout among the witches and de elves!
Is dis yourself, Mahs' Flo.? And is dis you,
Miss Lucia? I can't trus' my eyes no mo'!
But nothin's hurt me in dis haunted place.
I went to dat ole church a-huntin' you,
And de witch-music sot me off to sleep;
And den, I dremp, as I had gone to heaven,
A great, wide place, all thick wid shady trees,
Warm like a summer-day; and dere I saw—

Florian.

Nay, you shall tell your dream another time!
Round us there is a ring of lovely forms;
Look on them, Dan, and tell me what you see.

Dan.

Why, here I see the elf-child: mighty kind
She been to me dis night. I ain't afeard

Of her, nor dese here rosy, brown-skinned boys,
Wid furry ears like rabbits, quick black eyes,
And grape-and-ivy twisted round dere heads.

Rosemary.

The brownies and the fauns, these black-eyed boys,
Shall talk with you, and teach you many things.
Wild are they, and yet gentle; human-hearted,
Although their pointed ears are clad in fur.
These are not like gross fauns of olden time,
But frolic-loving spirits of the woods.
They love dumb creatures of the mother Earth,
And, among humankind, they love the meek,
The young, the helpless, and the ignorant.—
But is there nothing more that you can see?

Dan.

Nothin at all, cept my Mahs' Flo., and you,
Miss Lucia, if '*tis* you in dese wild woods.

Lucia.

Nay, see, good Dan, close standing at my side,
There is a lady with long, lovely hair,
And dewy-shining eyes, sweet smiling there;
Her robe, a lace like cobweb hung with dew,
And garments green as young wheat shining through.

Dan.

I see a fringe-tree hangin' in full tossel,
But spider-webs and ladies, not a mossel.

FLORIAN.

Do you not see the wreath about her hair
Shed sparks of light upon her tresses fair?
And the fine point of flame above her brow,
That all around her spreads a tender glow,
Like silver-softness of dissolving mist,
By the full moon to airy brightness kissed?

DAN.

I see de fox-fire's greenish kind o'spark,
And lightin'-bugs a shinin' in de dark.

FLORIAN.

O eyes, to such ethereal beauty blind!
But say, cannot you hear the fairy kind,
With airy flutes, and voices sweet and low,
And wingéd feet, that lightly come and go?
With ecstasy the air is thrilled and stirred.

DAN.

I hear de night-thrush and de mockin'-bird;
De frogs croak in de marsh, and now and den,
A hootin' owl dat's higher up de glen.

ROSEMARY.

If he cannot behold sweet Eglantine,
How can he see Fantasma's beauty shine?
His mortal frame is all unfit to bear
The purity of Fairyland's fine air:

For higher souls than his, and minds more clear,
Have shrunk from that supernal atmosphere.

REDBUD (FIRST BROWNY).

Leave him to us! In harmless revelry
Night's few remaining hours shall lightly flee;
And truths shall find their way to heart and brain,
Which he in his own world shall still retain.

SILVERLEAF (FIRST FAUN).

Come, Dan, we will not envy Fairyland,
When pleasures here are spread on every hand.
    We'll follow the wild-bee
To hidden sweets within the honey-tree;
We'll seek the fairest fruits our woods afford,
    And gather the wild-gourd,
Wherein the wine of elf-land shall be poured,
Which never clouds the brain, but warms the heart,
Till the last memory of pain depart.

REDBUD (FIRST BROWNY).

 And music you shall hear
 Fit for a monarch's ear,
From pipes of reeds most musical and clear;
 While our quick feet keep time
 Like smooth words in a rhyme,
Nor any evil thing shall venture near.
  [*Exeunt* Fauns *and* Brownies *with* DAN.

ROSEMARY.

Come, let the poet be with laurel crowned;
Let beauty's locks with asphodels be wound![1]
The milk-white flowers that speak of fadeless bloom,
In floral stars that light the forests' gloom:
Crown them, that so the cloudland's airy band
May lead them to Fantasma's magic-land.

[*As the* Fairies *crown* LUCIA *and* FLORIAN, *aerial music is heard, and the* Sylphides *descend.*]

THE QUEEN-SYLPH.

Behold the fairy car
  Whose splendor shines for you!
  It is made of ether blue,
It is wreathed with many a star,
  And the moonlight silvers through;
  And above it, bending, too,
The rainbow's triple bar—
  That most ethereal bow
  The night-skies sometimes show
  When the full moon pours her rays
  Through the night-rain's tender haze.

  Ascend the starry car!
We will guide it safely through
The land of clouds and dew,
  Like a newly risen star

Through the heavens' purple blue,
    To the Fairyland afar!
LUCIA *and* FLORIAN *ascend the car. The scene closes.*

SCENE III. *The Shore of the Fairy Sea. The Fairy Car descends with the* Sylph-Queen, LUCIA *and* FLORIAN.

        SYLPH-QUEEN.
Bright Lucia and fair Florian! lovely pair,
We have brought you safely through the realms of air,
    Through the dim cloudland winging
Our way to this enchanted sea,
Whence rise, in happy haste to welcome ye,
The sea-nymphs, moving to the melody
    Of waves in gladness singing.
And lo, the ocean-maidens bring you gifts!
See, where Ligeia[1] in both hands up-lifts
A carcanet into the light that shifts
    From point to point of the long trailing splendor;
Opal, and jacinth, and aqua-marine,
Coral, and lazulite, and almondine,
And fair as moonlit snow-drift's trembling sheen,
    Full-rounded pearls in pallid beauty tender.
And we, the sylphides, have bestowed on you
A gift more subtle than the ethereal blue,
More fair and fine than rainbows in the dew:
A gift ye both will see and understand,
Treading the fragrant lawns of Fairyland.

FLORIAN.

Air-dwelling spirit of the starlit eyes!
Must we, then, lose our gentle guardian here?
Why must we lose to gain some newer joy,
A dear, familiar bliss?

SYLPH-QUEEN.

                        In Fairyland
It is not so: we will re-join you there,
With fairies of the woodland and the mine.
[*The* Sylph *disappears. Soft music from under the sea:* LIGEIA
approaches the strand.]

LUCIA.

Child of the sea, out-stretching pearl-white hands,
Hands filled to overflowing with the gems
Whose close-linked splendors from thy fingers trail—
Is it for me, that most resplendent chain?

LIGEIA.

Thrice coiled about thy neck, belovéd maid!
   Not the gold spark upon thy brother's breast,
Nor thy rich girdle, nor the unfading braid
   Of fairy-blossoms wreathed about your brows,
   Can give you bliss more high than this bestows;
For, with this necklace, thou shalt be possessed
Of joy that will not fade, a heart in perfect rest!

(*To Florian.*)
   Take thou this charmèd lyre—
    'Twill make thee music's lord:
   Through the strings of silver wire
   Runs a subtle fairy fire,
    Refining every chord.
  (*A shooting-star flashes across the Sea.*)

Obey that star—a call to you and me!
Behold, the kindly moon has laid for thee
A bridge of pearl-and-silver on the sea,
  Fit for the foot-prints airy
Of the bright spirits of the cloud and star,
Who hither led your rainbow-circled car;
  Or for a woodland fairy,
Who would not wish in our green wave to dip
The downy plumelet of her pinion's tip.

  And you, if so ye will,
May walk upon this moon-laid bridge of pearl,
Nor fear the billow's roll, the eddy's whirl,
  For the charmed sea is still.

Or choose ye to lave your limbs in the wave,
  And sport with the sea maidens there?
We will shield you from harms with white-wreathèd arms,
  And the veil of our far-flowing hair.

Or, choose ye a beautiful boat,
The finest, the fairest afloat;
A lily that lies on the lake,
A shell from the depths of the sea—
Choose, and a shallop we'll make,
Whose motion shall melody be!

Lucia.
O yonder smiles enchanting Fairyland!
Sweet is the sea, and sweet the flowery strand,
And sweeter still, Fantasma's fairy band!

Florian.
The lovely spirits of the woodland bowers,
Their chaplets thick with many-colored flowers;
The snow-winged sylphs, with silver-sprinkled tiars;
The jeweled guardians of the central fires;
White-floating sirens, lilies of the sea,
Moving in time to their own melody,
Tossing round arms, and crinkling tresses spangled
With drops of spray, like sea-moss pearl-entangled!
[*Music floats over the Sea from the Fairy Islands. The Sea-Nymphs answer with harp and shell.*]

Ligeia.
See, in the whiteness of the full moon's smile,
Fantasma's fairy shallop leaves the isle;
A fluted shell, wreathed like an Argonaut,
    Bright as the sickle of the waning moon,

Radiant with luster from the morning caught,
    And trembling star-like on the still lagoon ;
Such is the splendor of this lucid shell,
    Lined with a golden light that through it beams,
Like fireflies in a lily's waxen cell ;
    The silver-silken sail above it gleams,
Sending to earth and air strange odor new,
    Sweeter than heliotrope in morning dew.

    Above the barque is bending
A halo of pale-golden lights,
    With mildest amber blending;
And, floating higher still, a band of sprites,
    Like Old-Worlds Cupids, flying
In double circles, scatter flowers,
Till, reddened by the perfumed showers,
    The quiet sea is lying,
Like a Titan who reposes
    'Neath a covering of roses.

    And the snowy swans that guide
    The shallop o'er the tide,
    Are the singing-swans of old ;
    And their notes of liquid gold
    Made the melting harmony
    That came floating o'er the sea.

    Now, the shallop nearer floats !
    Enter ye this boat of boats ;

While the fairy sprites above
Float, an airy ring of love,
In the smiling sea beneath,
We surround you, like a wreath
Of the water-lilies fair.
Merry spirits in the air,
Sound your softest melody—
We will answer from the sea!
And the swans therein will chime,
As their silver wings keep time,
Like the sweetness of a triple-ending rhyme.

[*Soft Music. As the boat conveys* LUCIA *and* FLORIAN *across the Sea, the Scene closes.*]

PART V.

SCENE I. *Fairyland. The Throne-Room in the Palace of Beauty.*

[FANTASMA *on her throne, attended by the* Fairy Court, ROSEMARY *and the* Hermit.]

FANTASMA.

Thou hast not seen the whole of Fairyland;
That could not be, in man's brief span; but much
Of new and strange hast thou beheld and heard.
What thinkest thou of my world of loveliness?

HERMIT.

Nay, spirit, ask me rather what I think
Of shapes that people Saturn; for I know
As much or more of that dim, distant world,
Than of this region thou call'st Fairyland.

FANTASMA.

What dost *thou* call it?

HERMIT.

Even as thou dost.
A land of 'wildering lights and witching shades;

World in a world; where strangely are commingled
Beauty and wisdom, virtue, mirth, and truth,
Wealth, charity, devotion, happiness;
Some of which things, wise men have ever taught
Were mortal to each other.

   FANTASMA.
      And why so?
Say, why should wisdom not be beautiful,
Or beauty wise?
   HERMIT.
    Grant that so much might be;
Can riot and religion dwell together?

   FANTASMA.
No! But religion may abide with joy.
Thrice blest is he in whom they dwell together;
Whose clear large soul is rich in faith; whose heart
Holds a continual feast of merriment.

   HERMIT.
This fine, strange air exhilarates like wine;
I see, as though I never saw before,
And unaccustomed thoughts are in my mind.
Most strange, that Beauty teaches sage Experience!

   FANTASMA.
GOD'S staves are "beauty and bands;"[1] but thou wouldst break
The first, and make the last an iron rod.

The best of men have made mistakes, but few
So deadly, and so passing strange as this:
To drive out Beauty from her Father's house,
So that she wanders homeless through the world,
(Her rightful empire), hated of her friends.
Triumphant Evil claims her as his own;
A claim as false as the great Source of falsehood;
For Evil is not beautiful, nor was,
Nor ever will be, while the ages roll.
Beauty is good, and Goodness beautiful!
Though the Snake's worshipers may call him seraph,
Though Sin wear beauty's mask—it *is* a mask,
And nothing more.   Beauty and sin are foes,
For holiness and beauty are but one.

HERMIT.

Perforce, I must admit the saying true.
A goodly and a glorious work art thou
Of the Supreme in goodness and in glory,
Fantasma, spirit of the beautiful!

FANTASMA.

Wilt thou not deign to be our guest awhile,
O reverend lover of all moral beauty?
We will become thy pupils; and thou, too,
May'st learn of us, despite thy time-touched hair.
Thy mortal knowledge, won from grief and pain,
Will strengthen our light souls with rich experience;
And we will teach thee very many ways,

More than thou know'st, to soothe the wounded heart,
Cheer the dark mind, and heal the stricken soul!

HERMIT.

Right gladly will I stay and learn of thee.
My soul is filled with new humility;
Humility, the sweetest virtue known
To man, and the least practiced!

FANTASMA.
                Honor's self
Walks hand in hand with sweet humility.
[*Triumphal music. Soft brilliant lights play through the Room. The fountains play. Enter* LUCIA *and* FLORIAN. *A shower of bright blossoms falls before them, as if thrown by invisible spirits in the air.*]
Come near, my best-beloved, my beautiful!
Kneel not to me—I will descend to you;
You and this holy Hermit, whom I love.
Of human kind, ye only are so blest
To press the magic soil with mortal feet,
Though oft your souls have dwelt in Fairyland.

LUCIA.

Dear and most wondrous spirit! Is the Hermit
Among thy lovers and thy friends, at last?

FLORIAN.

Lost in the bliss of simply being here,

I saw thee not, good father! Though I knew
Fantasma's gracious love had brought thee hither.

FANTASMA.

Hermit, thou seemest lost in pleasant dreams;
What most awakes thy wonder in my palace?

HERMIT.

Its beauty! Its surpassing excellence
Of beauty and of splendor!

FANTASMA.

           Thou see'st best
And clearest, what thy mind best apprehends.

HERMIT.

This vast hall, whence so many galleries lead,
Like a wide-branching cave whose starry roof
Rests on stalactites white as frozen snow;
The glittering columns, (garlanded with flowers
Whereon the springing fountains scatter dew),
Rise in long, shining ranks from the smooth floor,
Translucent, clear, and green as malachite,
Enriched with veins and spangles of bright gold.
Along the gleaming walls of lucent pearl
Run rich festoons and wreaths of glowing flowers,
Burning like jewels; and around them hover
Rich butterflies and birds of starry plumes.

FANTASMA.
And see'st thou nothing more to wake thy wonder?

HERMIT.
Too much! But, chiefly, thy resplendent throne,
A mass of precious stones—or, are they stars?
Mingling prismatic tints, like morning dew.
On either side, as they were jeweled statues,
A peacock stands, lifting, in graceful pride,
Lithe, lustrous neck and crested head superb.
The throne is shaded by a canopy
Made in the semblance of a passion-flower,
The great corolla's rayant fringes spread,
Round which there floats a ring of humming-birds.

LUCIA.
With ruby-glancing throat and flashing breast,
They keep one place, and hang on whirring wings,
Summer's sweet lovelings, quivering with delight.

FANTASMA.
So, poets, in their moving through the world,
Awake the sleeping harmony; sweet echoes
Of careless words and feet whose natural movement
The flattering world has called a poet's work.

FLORIAN.
O fairy work! Merely to breathe and be!

Lucia.

The Hermit looks upon the wondrous throne,
But brighter is the queen who sits thereon.
Wearing the emerald star above her brow!
Thy silvan crown, the sensitive vine, yet wreathes
The golden tendrils of thy floating hair,
With delicate flowers and plume-leaves dewy-wet,
Despite this lavish splendor; and the robe
Veiling thy matchless symmetry of shape,
Glows like the morning's blush through tender mist,
As rosy-silver as thine aureole.

Florian.

O beautiful Fantasma! Who dost bring
All rays of beauty into one bright ring,
As the sweet mocking-bird has made his own
All music that the vocal woods have known,—
Is it thy star wherein the witchery lies,
Or the soft splendor of those liquid eyes?
Is it the opal scepter gives command,
Or the white waving of that snow-soft hand?
Is it the words we hold our breath to hear,
Or tender tones that bless the charmèd ear?
Immortal beauty lights those features fair;
Unearthly splendor wreathes thy flame-gold hair;
No hue of earth upon that cheek doth dwell,
A crimson fire within a pearl-white shell;
And richer than the crimson of the cheek
Are the fine lips that even in silence speak,

Their every glowing curve and eloquent line
With fullest meaning fraught and dreams divine!

FANTASMA.

Come, let us walk among the balmy groves,
Soft vales, and moon-lit lawns of Fairyland.
Lucia and Florian, you shall go with me,
But the good Hermit needs an hour of rest.
Rosemary, lead him to those soft, low vales
Wherein my shepherds feed their snowy flocks.
Lead him beneath the shade of coffee-trees,
And let their berry yield its golden juice,
The cup of comfort.   Bring him carven bowls
Of satin-wood and cedar, brimmed with cream
And the rich beverage of the chocolate-tree.
Gather him bread-fruit from our Asian vales,
Fruit from the honey-locust, rich bananas,
Pomegranates, figs, and golden-dusted dates;
And, after, lull him into sweetest rest,
On cushions of clover-pinks and lavender.

HERMIT.

I thought, your realm had been the land of dreams;
The soul's retreat.   You have material pleasures?

FANTASMA.

Rosemary, where the changeling fairies dwell
Have they not gardens human-like and fair?

ROSEMARY.

There are soft vales, kept green by winding brooks,
    Along whose borders mint and cresses grow,
And calamus, and comfrey; in damp nooks
    The purple flag and azure iris blow;
    Hyacinths, with pink blossoms all a-row;
And there are banks with parsley overrun,
    And wild-thyme, trailing to the stream below;
Marjoram, sage, and basil, every one;
Sweet-fennel, nard, and rue; but evil weeds are none.

Here the narcissus opens cups of gold,
    And broad-leaf lilies on the waters rest;
Love-vines and bamboo, tangled in one fold
    O'errun the alders, shade the brooklet's breast;
    The trailing ivy, in full verdure dressed,
And trumpet-vines, and water-loving flowers;
    Green thickets, where the redbird builds his nest.
The little streams are lost among their bowers,
And greenly spread the meads, refreshed by frequent
    showers.

There grow green rosemary, and plumy tansy,
    And lavender, and fragrant celery;
Strawberries riot with the pink and pansy,
    In sweet confusion, beautiful to see,
    Because each grows by each harmoniously,
Nor kill each other, as poor earthly plants.
    Here, beauty, wedded to utility,

Not merely wears the cestus that enchants,
But bears the fruitful horn, supplying simplest wants.

There are fruit-laden orchards, spicy apples,
    Cherry, and plum, and rosy nectarine;
Pears, striped and flecked with green and ruddy dapples;
    Orange and citron, lemon, fig, and pine,
    And many a fair fruit from the glowing Line,
And vines, with black and golden clusters crowned,
    Pomegranates whose ripe seeds like garnets shine:
The over-laden branches kiss the ground
    Where tempting melons lie profusely all around.

    FANTASMA.

Lead thou the Hermit to those peaceful bowers,
That he may rest; for much has he to see,
To hear, and learn, ere he leaves Fairyland.
Come, Lucia, and my Florian, let us go
And mingle with my fays of bower and lawn.
Be not astonished, if you should behold
The buds of spring beside the fruits of fall;
We might, if we so willed it, mingle spring
With summer, autumn with the winter blend,
Braiding the year in one redundant wreath;
But for ourselves we seldom use this power;
Sweeter it is to follow Nature's law,
And take the rolling seasons as they come.

[*Rainbows flash from the fountains, that spring higher; and the rainbows, crossed and re-crossed, form an arch through which* FANTASMA, LUCIA, FLORIAN, *and attendant Fairies pass from the Hall:* ROSEMARY *leads away the* HERMIT *by another door. A dance of Fairies to gay music. The rainbows increase, crossing in soft confusion, till all grows indistinct, and the scene closes amid the play of lights and colors.*]

SCENE II. *The Pleasure Grounds of Fairyland:* FAIRIES, NYMPHS, &c. *Apart from the others,* FANTASMA, LUCIA, *and* FLORIAN.

LUCIA.

The moonlight falls, a liquid-silver flood,
    Filling the air with rapture sweet and strange;
Touching to fairy loveliness the wood,
    The flowery lawn, the distant mountain-range,
The streamlet, shining in its claritude.

FLORIAN.

Behold our shadows on the dewy ground!
Each head is with a saint-like glory crowned,
Like the anthelia of the Eastern isle,
When earth lies hushed in morning's rosy smile.
Is it the Fairyland's supernal light
That crowns our shadows with a wreath so bright?

FANTASMA.

That shining shade is but the reflex fair
    Of the invisible crown on you bestowed

By the ethereal fays of air and cloud,
The happy head that such a wreath doth wear
    Shall seldom by regret or grief be bowed;
Never by shame, never by sordid care.

Lucia.

This gift they said we could but understand
When breathing the fine air of Fairyland.

Fantasma.

Come, let us rest beside this dripping-spring,
    Beneath these soft mimosa-trees, that throw
    Such delicate shadows on the stream below;
Shadows more fine than fairy penciling.
This dropping fountain, with its silver ring,
    Lulls yet enlivens, with a witching spell,
    Because a spirit lives within the well:
My fairy realm contains no lovelier thing.

Florian.

May we not see this fairy of the fount?
    As kind as beautiful must be the sprite
Who drew these rillets from the azure mount,
    To make this well for Fairyland's delight.
The moonlight loves to strike across the rain
    Of twinkling drops, and a fine fairy bow
Appears, and disappears, and comes again,
    As clouds across the sweet moon come and go.

FANTASMA.

Fairy, arise! The moonlit skies
Smile like the tender light that lies
    On the silvery brow of dawn;
    And the dew on the daisied lawn
Is shining like the light of liquid eyes tear-bright!
    Sweet Claribel, arise!
Arise, O fountain sprite!
[*The* Fountain-Fairy *arises from the dripping-spring.*]

FLORIAN.

Phantasmal beauty! with transparent wings
    So crystal-clear they almost mock the sight,
    And hung with bells like lilies made of light!
And every tiny bell vibrating swings,
Chiming with the sweet fountain as it rings.

CLARIBEL.

    For thee I leave, O queen!
      My cool and crystal dwelling,
    Where waters, diamond-sheen,
      From emerald urns are welling.
Harken to my silver singing;
All my crystal bells are ringing,
    Ringing sweet,
    Ringing fleet,
Till all the echoes run on airy feet,
    Adown the balmy gale,
    Along the flowery vale,

Till the distant mountain sends me soft replies.
[*A Chime of Bells.*
I hear the hidden streams
   That feed my fairy fountain,
Awaking from their dreams
   In the echo-charmèd mountain,
Upspringing to my singing,
While my airy bells are ringing—
    Ringing low,
      Ringing slow,
Fading, fading, as I go;
   And when I disappear,
   The echoes, fine and clear,
Melt as softly as the music heard in dreams.
[*A chime of bells, growing softer as the Fairy disappears.*]

Lucia.

How strange, that music sweet as this should make
The spirits fail, the yielding mind grow sad!

Florian.

Yet did the echoes' fairy chimes awake
   Joy in my soul, so sweetly did they fade,
   Like falling waters in a distant glade,
Receding as the onward way we take.

Fantasma.

Nay, ye must not dream pensively to-night,
Whose coming has made Fairyland more bright;

For I would show you all the wonders here:
The splendid past shall to your sight be clear;
The bright creations of the painter's art,
Sculpture and poesy shall do their part;
In shapes most palpable and clear,
Long-lost poetic dreams for you shall re-appear,
And higher fancies, to the world more dear.
Whate'er ye will, shall rise above the wave
    Of time, though hidden there whole ages long:
    Choose—heroes, beauties, sages, saints among;
Divine Achilles, beautiful and brave,
    Or sad-eyed Lamia of a modern song.
But, one short hour will not suffice for this,
    And, when the morning comes, you must return
    To your own world, to labor and to mourn,
And to endure with patience all that is
    Apportioned to a spirit shut in clay,
    Till death shall take the prison-bars away.
                               [*A mocking-bird sings.*

FLORIAN.

O matchless songster! never fairy grove
    Could add more sweetness to the liquid note
    That flows like golden honey from thy throat,
When, singing to the moon thy passionate love,
    Those witching strains through some lone chamber float,
And melt the soul misfortune could not move.
                                 [*A Fairy-Bird sings.*

Lucia.

Hark! Sweeter, sadder song was never heard!
Is it the night thrush, or the mocking-bird?
Is it an oriole, singing in the dark?

Florian.

Too sad it is for oriole or for lark.
How softly did the sweet sounds flow and fail!
Is it the love-desiring nightingale?

Lucia.

Nay, list! The same sweet bird begins again.

Florian.

It is no bird, for words distinct and plain
Are fitted to the full, melodious strain.

[*The* Fairy-Bird *sings.*]
How oft I've heard the mocking-bird
    His soul in music pouring,
When earth lay white in trancing light
    Of a silent night in June!
The tuberose and the bird, in sweetness soaring,
    The queen of night adoring,
    With passionate imploring:
        "O thou, serene and lonely!
        I love—I love thee only!
        I love thee—love thee only,
Thou sweet and silent moon!"

FLORIAN.
That is the echo of a German song;
I knew and loved it when I was a child.
Whatever sung this song, it was no bird.

LUCIA.
It wears the shape, at least, of a bright bird,
As fair as flitted through the groves of Eden.
It sits upon a spray of that green ash
That droops its tasseled branches by the stream.
O beautiful beyond the birds of earth!
How rich its plumes of emerald and gold,
And orange-glowing throat, like living flame!
It's splendid train would shame a peacock's pride;
And on the delicate head it bears a crest
Shaped like a lyre and shining like fine gold,
The delicate plumelets trembling at a breath.

FLORIAN.
What is the name of this strange, beautiful bird?

FANTASMA.
This song-bird once dwelt in your own fair world.
He woke to life among the mocking-birds .
Of Southern lands, but was no mocking-bird.
Companion he had none in all the grove,
But lonely ever was, and sometimes sad.
He heard the music of the singing-swans
Borne on the east winds from a distant land,

And then he sought companionship with them;
But they rejected the wild wanderer.
And so he flew away to Fairyland,
Because he found no friend in all the world.
Would you behold the shape he wears on earth?
For, still the clay-born body must remain
On earth, till death shall give it rest. Take, Lucia,
This opal wand of mine, and with it touch
The bird's reflection in the glassy stream.

[*As* Lucia *touches the Shadow, the bird disappears, and the* Phantasm *of a dark-haired* Youth *arises from the water.*]

Behold, this phantom wears an aureole
Worn only by the high-souled and the pure.
Before the bird sang, he had fallen asleep
Within a garden which he tends by day;
And when he sleeps, the unresting soul takes wing,
Hasting to Fairyland, where that bright bird
Receives it; and my spirits love it well.
Eidolon! Sing to us, that these may learn
How happiness descends like clouds of dew
Upon the soul that draws its bliss from heaven.
Sing them the thought that soothed you ere you slept.

Phantasm.

The evening wind breaks up the light upon the shining river;
    It wakes the solemn music in the ever-sounding pines;
It sweeps across the garden, and the bending roses quiver,
        And the trellised arbor trembles in its wreathing trumpet vines.

And from the boughs of shaken trees, whereby the light wind passes,
    The dew-drops and the fire-flies came down in starry showers:
Fire-flies floating in the air, and flashing from the grasses;
    Dancing, darting everywhere, and lighting up the flowers.

Let indoor students ponder deep into the midnight stilly;
    I cannot read my lesson by the light their lamp supplies;
The glimmer of a flame-fly in the white cup of a lily,
    Is a light that's better suited to a poet's dreaming eyes.

I would not barter places with the trader or the schemer;
    I envy not the stronger minds their honors or their gold;
More useful they may be than I, the poet and the dreamer:
    I would not take from higher hearts a single gift they hold.

They do not see what shines for me in blossom or in berry;
    The mocking-bird sings not for them the song he sings for me;
The silver on a poplar leaf,[1] the coral of a cherry,
    Is rich as any mine of earth or jewel of the sea.

What though no word of love or praise the world to me may render?
    The God who heard the choral stars that hailed a planet's birth,

Is the same who made the mocking-bird and praised the lily's
　　　splendor;
　　He will find a use for poets in a wider realm than earth.

O Father of the universe! I tremble and adore Thee!
　　I thank Thee for the ears that hear, and for the eyes that
　　　see ·
The pulsing harmonies of earth, her beauty and her glory!
　　I thank Thee for the gift of life—the soul that turns to
　　　Thee!
[*As the* Phantasm *fades, soft music from the fountain mingles
　with the mocking-bird's song. The scene closes.*]

SCENE III. *Another Part of Fairyland, near the Sea.* FAN-
　　TASMA, LUCIA, *and* FLORIAN.

FANTASMA.
The hour is fast approaching when we part,
　　For but a little while, for ye will come
To visit me, belovèd of my heart!
　　To learn the lessons of my fairy home,
To find deep truths in simple things, in nature and in art.

Remember, in the world to which ye go,
　　That good with evil must contend awhile;
To love is often better than to know;
　　To weep is sometimes sweeter than to smile.
Though ye may be beguiled, do not beguile;

Deceit is not the parent of success;
Achieve no victory by unworthy wile;
Hypocrisy knows naught of happiness,
But, if ye weep for others' woe, ye will not smile the less.

Your earth has many hours of rest and bliss,
And her strength-giving "fountain of the sun;"
And ye, arising from its sparkling bath,
Will seek no selfish joy, nor sorrow shun,
Nor from life's duties ever prove remiss,
Nor lose your fairy gifts, as some have done,
Who, self-sufficing, wandered from the path,
And lost themselves in labyrinths, where guiding clue was none.

And, every full-moon ye shall come to me,
The mysteries of my fairy realm to learn;
To dream within the Vale of Nephele,
Where amaranthine blooms like jewels burn;
To drink nepenthe from a starry urn;
To read strange scrolls of long-forgotton lore;
To taste the fruit of immortality,
Till Death the angel shall be feared no more,
And Love, and Hope, and Faith, beam brighter than before.

Behold! The woodland fairies wait on ye,
The silver-crownèd sylphs are in the air,
The white armed sirens float upon the sea,

And from the inner caverns re-appear
The fire-sprites with their jewels in their hair.
> Listen, beloved, to these, and their sweet counsel hear.

Fire-Sprites.

O guard the lamp within your keeping placed,
> The vestal flame committed to your care!—

Loose not the serpent-zone about your waist;
> Love never had such girdle as you wear.

Wood-Fays.

Do not entwine the poisoned ivy-wreath
> Around the fadeless laurels we have given.—

The asphodel of life may turn to death,
> Unless its blossoms drink the dews of heaven.

Sea-Nymphs.

To no false worship, no unworthy strain,
> Awake the burning chords of thy rich lyre.—

Dim not the luster of thy jeweled chain,
> Nor sully with false breath its fairy fire.

Sylphs.

O never let the mist of earthly cloud
> The heaven-born splendor of your crowns obscure!

Seldom on mortals is such gift bestowed,
> And only on the faithful and the pure.

ALL.

Go, happy twain! and when the full-moon smiles,
Return again to bless the Fairy Isles.

[*A fine Cloud arises from the East, and dissolving to a silver Shower, falls into the Sea.*]

FANTASMA.

These are the gentle spirits of the dew,
    Who spend their charmèd nights upon the earth.
    Now, they return into their place of birth,
The sea, which ever doth their lives renew.
    And yonder, see, where shines the golden East,
Whose long, bright glance across the ocean strikes!
    Even now, the glowing splendor is increased,
And flames aloft in rosy-golden spikes.
    My fairy isles in moonlight ever lie,
    But o'er thine own bright world the sun is high.

The golden bridge is waiting for your feet;
    It flames across the smooth and burnished sea;
Farewell, awhile, my beautiful, my sweet!
    And in due time ye shall return to me.
Go, now, in sweet obedience; linger not,
    Nor backward glance; but, moving to the light,
Pass through the gateway by the morning wrought!
    And be your path through your own world as bright!

[LUCIA *and* FLORIAN *move Eastward over the Sea, to the Golden Arch.*]

LIGEIA.

Behold those lovely children of the earth
Along the track of morning lightly move,
As if their feet were shod with fairy gold!

FANTASMA.

Faith wings their feet, and makes the pathway firm.
O may they never leave the shining way!

There is a way that seemeth right,
Yet it leadeth down to death.
    Many ways the wide world hath ;
Hard it is to know the right ;
    Hard it is to choose the path
Leading always to the light.

CHORUS OF FAIRIES.

    Let the morning-star of Faith
    With the dawning Truth unite,
Till the kindling world arise slowly from engulfing night.

FANTASMA.

There is a wisdom that appears divine,
    So gracefully she wears the casque
That on true Wisdom's brow did shine :
    There is a beauty in whose false light bask
Strong souls and high, drunk with Circèan wine,
    Who neither know themselves nor her; nor ask
Where grew the blooms that in her garlands twine,
    Nor what the face beneath the beauteous mask ;

Nor at false wisdom's vile commands repine,
  But hasten to fulfill the unhallowed task,
And life, and love, and hope, into such hands resign.

Chorus.

Arise, O heaven-born Beauty! in thy might!
Disarm the false one of thy stolen light,
And shed o'er all the earth thy rays benign!

We hail thee, Beauty, chosen bride of Truth!
We love thee in the rosy smiles of youth,
And in the silver light of agèd hair!
Earth to her inmost heart is glad for thee!
Thou smilest in the green depths of the sea;
Thou fillest all the azure realm of air;
Thou ever wert, and must forever be,
Child of the universal King, the One supremely fair!

End of Fantasma.

NOTES TO FANTASMA.

PART I—Scene I.

1. "*A whippowil cries.*"

As this bird is named from its long, plaintive cry, the name should be spelled as above. The *sound* is not "whip-poorwill," but distinctly "whip-po-*wil!*" with emphasis on the ultimate.

2. "*We'll bofe be tricked.*"

That is, will be bewitched; will have a spell cast over us.

Scene II.

1. "*To follow any Jack-ma-Lanter's light.*"

Such is (or was) the negro's pronunciation of Jack-o'-Lantern, which he believed to be sometimes a merry, elfish boy, a good-natured but mischievous Puck; but, more frequently, imagined him an old, dwarfish man, preternaturally ugly and cruel, having a thick suit of crinkled, bushy hair.

2. "*Same as de fox-fire.*"

The phosphorescent gleam of decayed wood. The "isinglass" referred to by Dan is the mica, glittering in specks on the ground.

PART II—Scene I.

1. "*And the mocking-bird and tender thrush.*"

The night-thrush, a relative of the mock-bird; a sweet singer, but not a mimic; sings chiefly in the early part of night; well-known, of course, to naturalists, but very little known or appreciated by the people.

PART III—Scene I.

1. "*A canopy of grape and muscadine.*"

The muscadine is, of course, a grape; the Scuppernong in its wild state; but so much more beautiful, as a vine, than any other grape, that it is always spoken of as quite distinct from wild-grapes in general, some varieties of which are poisonous.

2. "*Green bamboo.*"

An evergreen brier, of which the young shoots are very slender, tough, and thornless.

3. "*Ivy-blooms.*"

Flowers of the common kalmia, a laurel called "wild-ivy" in the South.

4. "*Mocking-bird in moonlight singing.*"

It is well-known that mocking-birds sing on the wing, and are peculiarly restless in moonlight, as if exhilarated.

5. *" Woodbine."*

That is, the wild coral-honeysuckle.

6. *" I found the wild cucumber-tree."*

The *Magnolia Tripetala,* called, in Piedmont Virginia and Carolina, marsh-magnolia, cucumber, or umbrella-tree.

Scene IV.

1. *"Water-Nymphs and Sirens."*

These (it is scarcely necessary to say) are not the *classic* nymphs or sirens. The names of Grecian myths have been appropriated, for want of better, to the use of the phantasms of the New World.

Part IV—Scene II.

1. *" Let beauty's locks with asphodels be wound."*

The asphodel here meant is a Southern wild flower, so called: white, star-shaped, fragrant.

Scene III.

1. *" Ligeia."*

The name of a siren has been given to the queen of these New-World mermaids and naiads because of the beautiful *meaning* of this musical name. No other could be so appropriately borne by the queen of fairies presiding over seas, lakes, and all water-courses.

PART V.—Scene I.

1. "*Beauty and bands.*"

"I took unto me two staves; the one I called Beauty, and the other I called Bands; and I fed the flock."—*Zechariah, the Prophet; XI chapter, VII verse.*

Scene II.

1. "*The silver on a poplar-leaf.*"

That is, the silvery gleam on the under side of leaves of the tulip-tree, or tulip-poplar.

THE LIGHT-BRINGER:

IN TWO PARTS.

PREFACE.

To Mrs. L. R. M., Kansas City, Mo.

1.

How many a moment I owe thee
  Of exquisite rest and pure pleasure!
    And what can I give in return?
What fairy-blessed gift can I show thee?
  What genie will bring me a treasure
    High-heaped in a long-buried urn,
Rare gems and red gold beyond measure?

2.

Not gold thou desirest, nor jewel;
  My friendship is thine in completeness.
    So naught can I give thee but rhyme!
Yet, the spring-beauty's yearly renewal
  Is the same in its brightness and fleetness,
    And the birds of the new summer-time
Sing the old songs with ever-new sweetness;

3.

So, take the old words with new meaning:
  I can but repeat them with changes,—
    "I trust," "I esteem," or, "I love."—

And aceept this light sheaf of my gleaning
  In fields beside lone-lying granges,
    In forest and fay-haunted grove,
And the rifts of the mountain's wild ranges.

4.

A sheaf? Call it, rather, a garland,
  With grasses and wild-growing lilies
    And weeds intermixed as they come:
As a wanderer culls in a far land
  Mementos that show what his will is,
    And gifts for the loved ones at home,
That tell where the clinging heart still is.

5.

And true love meets never with scorning,
  Though small be the gifts of its sending;
    Nor wilt *thou* my garland disdain:
Although it may lack the adorning
  Of fancy and taste interblending,
    So carelessly twined and so plain,—
Thy kindness will give it commending.

MAY 2, 1879.

PROEM.

I.

The house of Silverlinn was large and tall,
    With two great wings spread out on either side;
Old-fashioned, rambling, picturesque withal;
    Its neighbors' envy and its owner's pride:
An oaken stair ran round the great square hall;
    Some rooms mere closets; others, long and wide;
Long corridors, and airy balconies;
Verandas, opening on green shrubberies.

II.

The ground in front was level as a floor,
    Being on the very summit of a hill,
Shaded by noble tulip trees that bore
    Their budding blossoms bravely; fairer still,
A great magnolia stood beside the door.
    The rear-ground fell by gentle slopes, until
It curved to meet the forest, on whose edge
The boundary fence was a trim cedar-hedge.

III.

Upon the left, the rolling lands were made
    Into a park-like garden, trimly kept;

Where saucy squirrels in the oak-trees played,
 And swans across the lovely lakelet swept,
White as the lilies growing in the shade
 Of willows that above the waters wept;
And wild-ducks preened their plumage in the stream
Where sportive trout flashed with a silver gleam.

IV.

Upon the right, the picture well might please
 A painter's eye, the wild, romantic scene
Of art and nature: flower-sown terraces
 Descended sharply to a deep ravine,
A torrent's bed; and, rich in waving trees,
 Beyond, the mountain reared its wall of green,
A background for the stream whose foamy flow
Sprang from a cliff to the ravine below.

V.

From this wild cataract the whole domain
 Was named, with some propriety; for still
The silver-sparkling waterfall's refrain
 Awoke the mountain echoes, clear and shrill,
As, twisting, twinkling like a silver chain,
 It flashed and foamed along the parent-hill,
Till its last leap, from the great rocky wall,
Changed it to silvery gauze in one long fall.

VI.

Fronting this waterfall, a pleasant room
    Opened upon the terrace: here, among
Papers and books, the planter sat, to whom
    Did Silverlinn and its demesnes belong;
Near him, a guest in manhood's early bloom;
    Smooth cheek and sparkling eye declared him young
Yet in the locks of wavy chestnut lay
Thick-sprinkled threads of most untimely grey.

VII.

This mingling of old age and blooming youth
    Half marred the face that nature formed so fair:
Though clear the dark-grey eye, the forehead smooth,
    Something there was that told of thought and care.
Half proud, half sad was the expressive mouth;
    A gentle voice he had, and courteous air;
Sharp were the outlines of the pure Greek face,
The supple form had strength allied to grace.

VIII.

The face with recent illness now was thin,
    For when to this lone valley first he came,
(Where, on the western slope stands Silverlinn),
    A subtle fever wasted all his frame;
And scarcely had his host the art to win
    The youth from death, or the wild pulses tame:
But no plain countryman was Charles Devane,
Who nursed young Calvert thro' those days of pain.

IX.

Now he was convalescent, though still weak,
    Languid, and in recovering very slow:
Too large the eyes, too pale the waxen cheek,
    Except when came the bright but transient glow,
As momentary as the lightning's streak,
    Or blush of sunset fading from the snow.
But he was stronger, on this April-day,
For the fresh air was balmy-mild as May.

X.

Devane the planter sat beside his guest,
    Smiling to see the color and the light
Rise, like the first faint dawning of the East,
    To the large, languid eye, and cheek so white.
Of all his friends, Devane had loved the best
    Young Calvert's father, when their youth was bright.
Fast friends at school, their friendship closer grew
In all the after-time, their whole life through.

XI.

But Howard Calvert dwelt beside the Bay,
    The blue-waved Chesapeake's unresting tide;
While in the shadow of the Blue Ridge lay
    Devane's inheritance, his love and pride.
Then Calvert went to foreign lands away;—
    But time nor distance could these friends divide.
The old man opened heart and house to one
Beloved for Calvert's sake—his only son.

XII.

Some sixty years the planter might have seen;
    Of figure slightly built, but somewhat low;
A pleasant voice; a mild and winning mien;
    Dark, brilliant eyes, beneath a calm, broad brow;
Locks wintry white, yet soft and silken sheen;
    Long-flowing beard, a drift of fleecy snow:
His face was kindly touched by time and care;
His heart as fresh as his own mountain-air.

XIII.

Still talked Devane, but, with an absent mind,
    Calvert sat musing in his secret breast:
"How little did I hope," he thought, "to find
    A second father, coming as a guest
Unknown! To him confessed, to be here resigned
    The secret grief which has so long oppressed,
Almost destroyed. But, yet—can I depend
Even on *his* faith, the true and trusted friend

XIV.

"Of my dead parents? True, and worthy trust;
    Faithful, and yet—but human, nevertheless!
And, should he cast me off, it were but just,
    Nor could he know my utter wretchedness.
The good sometimes forget that they are dust.
    Could one so pure sin's lightest torture guess?
Can I, so dark a sinner, hope to win
Pity from one who justly hates the sin?

XV.

"In silence I must bear my heavy load.
    I *will* retain the trust of this great heart!
Conscience may lash me, and remorse may goad—
    I will not shun, nor seek to salve the smart;
But I will walk alone on this dark road:
    My only comforter must be my art."
He sighed aloud, and starting, met the eyes
Of his kind host, fixed on him with surprise.

XVI.

"Are you in pain, my son?" the old man asked.
    Calvert, with some embarrassment said "No!"
And, by an effort of the strong will, masked
    His features in tranquillity; but, though
His shrewd old host was not deceived, he tasked
    His skill to make the conversation flow,
When suddenly these words from Calvert burst:
"By whom, in my delirium, was I nursed?"

XVII.

"By me and little Eulis, till so wild
    You grew, my niece was frightened: in her stead
A trusty servant came. I see, my child,
    You are uneasy, lest you may have said
Something you might regret;" the old man smiled,
    As Calvert started, flushing burning-red.
"But be at ease! Wild, 'whirling words' you spoke;
Nothing coherent, till your reason woke."

XVII.

Then Edwin Calvert took the planter's hand,
  So strong, so skillful, yet so delicate.
"The life that you have saved, you may command,"
  He said. "The stranger whose unhappy fate
Still kept him wandering from land to land
  Will bless the day that saw him pass your gate,
True friend, so strong, so tender and benign—
My father's friend, and oh! how truly mine!"

XIX.

"You told me you loved pictures," said Devane;
  "And as most pleasures must be still denied,
Perhaps these drawings you may like to scan:
  See, here is Silverlinn, my special pride,
Sketched by a wandering painter, a young man
  Resembling you." The smiling youth replied;
"I, also, am a landscape-painter: you,
Who love the art, should love the artist, too."

XX.

"Even as I love myself," the planter said,
  Smiling. "I was a painter in my youth,
And dreamed of rivaling the glorious dead,
  The Masters; but I did not find it smooth,
The road to fame! Both hope and fancy fled;
  I ceased to look for light or seek for truth
Save that God gave his children. Life, to me,
Is merely waiting for the life to be.

XXI.

"Of all the gifts this world has to bestow,
    I sought Fame only: wealth I did not crave,
And love I scarcely heeded; even so,
    Pleasure was spurned: I was ambition's slave.
But GOD, the Maker, HE must surely know
    What are the fittest gifts that we should have:
Though that for which I panted was denied,
He gave me love, and wealth, and all beside.

XXII.

"I grieved, on seeing others take the place
    For which I strove; those who did not possess
My talent or my energy, found grace:
    It was decreed—the greater serve the less,
And careless runners passed me in the race.
    But when I saw the sacred laurels press
Unworthy brows amid the world's acclaim,
I sought no more the venal smiles of fame.

XXIII.

"But my one talent—I still keep it bright.
    That is not buried which is not displayed,
Nor is it lost, though hidden from the light,
    As pallid fruits that ripen in the shade.
And I have learned to love my art aright,
    As a kind household spirit, giving aid
In time of trouble, soothing all my pain,
And cheering me to take up life again.

XXIV.

"I tell you this, my son, because I feel
    That you have suffered; *how*, I do not know,
Nor wish to know the grief you would conceal:
    But my own disappointed life will show,
That, like the temper of the finest steel,
    True strength, true manhood, from submission flow.
If peace and *true* success you would secure,
First gain, my son, the power to endure."

XXV.

Calvert looked up with wild and startled eyes,
    Half questioning, half grateful; but remained
Silent, as if, beyond the mere surprise,
    There was a something in the words that pained.
Devane spoke lightly: "As you may surmise,
    I am a painter, still; and, now you've gained
The strength to walk so far, you'll smile to see
The studio that is worth a world to me."

XXVI.

They went through hall and passage merrily,
    Till, at a door, the planter paused, and said:
"Be not surprised at anything you see,
    And though you meet a monster, feel no dread;
For many curious things herein there be!"
    Laughing he spoke, nodding his fine grey head;
Then opened wide the door: its threshold crossed,
The youth stood, in amaze and horror lost.

XXVII.

The apartment was in shape an octagon,
    Lighted by one great window overhead:
Four of the sides were snowy-white, whereon
    Were painted roses, wreathed and garlanded;
The other sides were painted every one
    Like windows, with fine curtains overspread;
And through these seeming casements did the eye
Catch lovely views of mountain scenery.

XXVIII.

These four fine landscapes, painted on the wall,
    Were alternated with the other four,
The white-and-rose-decked sides of that strange hall:
    But Calvert, standing in the open door,
Gazed on an object startling more than all—
    A monster serpent, coiled upon the floor,
His oval rings piled upward, fold on fold,
A mass of mingling tints and gleams of gold.

XXIX.

This startling object, in the centre laid
    Of the apartment, let it be confessed,
Was not a snake, at all, but cushions made
    Of silk and velvet, fitting to be pressed
By some good genius, into sleep betrayed,
    Or fair sultana in her hour of rest:
And from the serpent's high-crowned head there swung
A basket, whence long leaves and blossoms hung.

XXX.

Upon this couch was laid the sleeping form
    Of a young girl, with blossoms garlanded,
Bright as the Indian Cupid:[2] soft and warm
    Glowed on her velvet cheek the dusky red;
Her drooping head lay on a rounded arm,
    O'er which the black and silky ringlets spread;
The crimson bodice seemed to sink and swell
When to her breath her bosom rose and fell.

XXXI.

This fairy-beauty was in age thirteen;
    The darling and the plague of Silverlinn:
An orphan girl, Devane had stood between
    The world and this lone child: once taken in
To heart and home, she ruled there, like a queen,
    Yet all her subjects' love contrived to win.
Calvert had heard of Eulis, and had heard
Eulis, herself, sing like a mocking-bird,

XXXII.

In the long halls, and from the garden-bowers
    Beneath his window, while so ill he lay;
Her fresh, young voice, heard in those languid hours,
    Had often charmed his weariness away;
And Eulis sometimes sent him gathered flowers;
    But he had never seen her till this day,
When, like the Eastern god, with flower-crowned head,
Sleeping she lay upon her serpent bed.

XXXIII.

This was a striking picture, strange but fair;
    Yet *horror* seemed the chief emotion raised
In Calvert's bosom—horror and despair,
    As, for one moment, fixedly he gazed,
With fear and loathing blent in one wild stare;
    Then fell, as lightning struck. Devane, amazed,
Called out for help: up sprang the sleeping child,
And thither ran the servants, scared and wild.

XXXIV.

"He is not dead, but swooning;" said Devane.—
    The servants bore young Calvert to his bed,
From which, indeed, he did not rise-again
    Until a week of suffering had fled:
Then sent he for his host: "I would explain
    The causes of my strange relapse;" he said.
"To you my whole strange life will I unfold,
My father's friend! To you shall all be told!"

XXXV.

In vain the planter begged him to defer
    His story, till his strength should quite return.
"Kind friend, seek not the wretched to deter
    From his fixed purpose. Haply, I may earn
Your sympathy, your pity: I will err
    No more through shame! My whole life you shall learn.
Shut fast the door, that none may enter in,
While I confess my sorrow and my sin.

XXXVI.

"You wondered at my weakness, I presume,
    In swooning on the threshold of your hall,
So strangely decorated; but that room
    So vividly and strangely did recall
An Eastern dwelling, where I sealed my doom—
    But I anticipate. You shall know *all!*
Listen, with patience: You behold in me
The hero of a true 'Soul's Tragedy.'"

PART I.

CANTO I.

I.

You know the story of my childish years,
    For most were spent, in pleasure, at your side.
My childhood knew much more of smiles than tears;
    Noted I was for frankness and for pride;
And I was wiser than my childish peers,
    A wayward elf, whose will was hard to guide:
I lived two lives—one, wild, and frank, and free;
The other, shut in dreams and mystery.

II.

My father was of Catholic descent;
    Of coldest Puritan blood my mother came;
And in their son were both these natures blent:
    Mine was the melting heart, the soul of flame;
And mine, too, was the calm, clear reason, meant
    To guide the soul and keep the passions tame:
And ere I knew the word philosophy,
I looked on life with philosophic eye.

III.

Strong was the brain; but all too highly strung,
    Too finely tuned the delicate chords of soul.
The mind was old, while heart and soul were young,
    And reason warred with want of self-control;
Almost I was like him by poets sung,
    Who first the sacred fire ethereal stole,
So was I vulture-torn and passion-riven,
Hanging midway betwixt the earth and heaven.

IV.

And yet, my soul was young, as I have said:
    Mine was the frank heart of a gleeful child;
A heart that ever fought against the head,
    In its free impulse, innocent, though wild.
Though much I pondered, and much more I read,
    Faith was not yet by subtlety beguiled,
Though Stygian streams embittered learning's well,
And nightshade grew beside the asphodel.

V.

The Muses life's divine elixir poured:
    Great Shakspere[1] laid his hand upon my heart,
And Homer struck the long-resounding chord:
    And England's matchless Egotist, whose art
Re-set the gems Antiquity had stored,
    And made the angels play a mortal part,
On the high altar hands presumptuously laid,
And entered in the Holiest, undismayed;—

VI.

He, whose magnificent audacity
    Has blinded thousands, to the present hour;
Many who fear their Maker cannot see
    How much this mortal's verse has dared to lower
Even *man's* conception of the ETERNAL THREE:
    With brow unbent before the awful Power,
He stalked with echoing step and changeless cheek,
And taught the Eternal GOD like man to speak.

VII.

I not enumerate the laureled throng
    Whose nectar-mantling chalices I drained;
But the sweet singer of a modern song
    Allured me most, and held my fancy chained:
To him the prophet's woe did well belong,[2]
    Denounced against a soul so deeply stained,
A mind so sin-distraught, it understood
The good for evil, evil for the good.

VIII.

The bitter he called sweet, the darkness, light;
    And dashed himself against the Almighty shield,
The finite striving with the Infinite;
    Sin, raving-mad, against all goodness steeled:
With what compassion must Immortal Might
    Have viewed that writhing soul, to sorrow sealed—
A soul that into darkness strayed so far
The Snake he worshiped for the Morning-Star!

IX.

Such was he, but not such to me he seemed,
    For then I scarcely thought an angel higher
Than he whose song so heavenly-sweet I deemed,
    Who swept with delicate hand the full-toned lyre;
Its sentient chords like rays of morning beamed,
    All wreathed about with unterrestial fire:
Alas! No coal from God's pure altar came
To touch those lips or gild that lyre with flame!

X.

He was my childhood's idol. I not knew,
    While eagerly the golden fruit I tasted,
From what foul roots that tree ambrosial grew:
    Full many an hour beneath its shade I wasted,
Nor knew its rich perfume and honey-dew
    All wholesome fruit whatever shrunk and blasted.
Well was my folly paid in future pain,
In sickened soul, and truth-distorting brain.

XI.

My youth was passed in Europe, as you know;
    In England part, and part in Germany.
I had three friends: no matter where or how
    I met them—they were all in all to me.
One was a German, but the other two
    Were English-born: we, four in unity,
Were members of a secret brotherhood,
Whose object was "the universal good:"

XII.

Meaning thereby, the turning upside-down
    And wrong-side-out, of all things, high and low:
Labor should rest, and wear a silken gown;
    Taxes should cease, and purses overflow;
There should be no such word as king or crown;
    No priest should live to prophesy of woe;
Churches should be pulled down, and all should be
Sweet Freedom and divine Equality.

XIII.

Arnstein was ultra-atheist in his views:
    To Comte, and then to Schopenhauer inclined,
He as his metaphysics grew abstruse,
    Left all men and all systems far behind.
"Philosophers and priests alike confuse;"
    He said: "The lamp of man is his own mind;
Who walks in others' paths goes more astray
Than he who wanders where there is no way."

XIV.

McCartney was Darwinian, for he had
    A mind with speculation all a-stir.
His mind than Arnstein's was of lower grade
    But brighter: a light-souled philosopher,
He welcomed Darwin's theory:[3] "Very glad,"
    He said, "with science always to concur."
A soul? McCartney felt no need of one,
And, for himself, was certain he had none.

XV.

Shirley was last and youngest of our band,
    And, of the four, at once the worst and best.
He had a poet's eye, a painter's hand;
    His genius could all trivial things invest
With a sweet glamour as of fairy-land;
    He seemed a wanderer from the stars; a guest
Of this dim world, where he remained awhile,
To dazzle, to instruct, and to beguile.

XVI.

His features would have been effeminate,
    But for the smoldering fire in his dark eye.
To me, he seemed a spirit good and great
    As ever walked beneath an alien sky;
I served him with devotion passionate,
    An idol, wrapped about with mystery.
They called him "atheist,"—but to me 'twas known
He had some strange religion of his own.

XVII.

'Tis certain, he possessed strange powers and arts;
    The wills of other men could bend and sway,
Reading the very secrets of their hearts:
    And oft he would sit poring night and day,
O'er strange, old maps, and long-forgotten charts,
    Or scrolls, writ in a language passed away.
He stood high in the "Mystic Brotherhood,"
And aimed, like them, at universal good.

XVIII.

For me—I speak in all humility—
    I was an earnest seeker for the truth,
No set supporter of a theory,
    Nor License woo'd for liberty: in sooth,
The florid charms of license pleased not me,
    Too much in earnest for the faults of youth:
And, Renan-like, I thought The Truth to find
By the pale glow-worm of a human mind.

XIX.

Whence had I come, and whither should I go?
    Was there an omnipresent Deity
To whom the small and great are like in show,
    Before the Infinite fading equally?
A Spirit, filling space, yet stooping low
    To shield the smallest creature—even me!
Was He a Father, good as infinite,
Or a dread form of overwhelming Might?

XX.

Was He all-wise, all loving, all foreseeing?
    Or built He in blind Power the universe,
Which had outgrown his grasp, and, ever-fleeing
    Down the dark future, grew from bad to worse,
Envolving tendencies which the great Being
    Who made, could not control? Was this the curse,
Or something darker, which was withering
The earth with sin, and blasting everything?

XXI.

If God has been offended, how can He,
    The Infinite, with us be reconciled?
Can He be reached, at all, by prayer or plea?
    Has He abandoned earth to the wide wild
Of chance, so that each soul must ever be
    A Fatherless, though an immortal child?
Such questions, and far more, in agony
I asked, and asked—but none could make reply:

XXII.

At least, no answer with conviction fraught.
    I had refused my parents' humble creed,
And though from pious priests at first I sought
    Guidance, they gave me little help, indeed;
I could not comprehend the faith they taught—
    For God alone can give the light we need
In seeking him. Thus, baffled every way,
I wandered, and in darkness went astray.

XXIII.

But my three friends and I were young and bright,
    Soaring aloft on hope's Icarian wings:
We called ourselves the "Seekers of the Light;"
    "Lovers of Truth;" and other pleasant things.
Each thought himself the true, invincible knight,
    Able to sweep the earth of priests and kings;
Each to dethrone the King of Heaven was bent,
And set up Demogorgon president.

XXIV.

While I was in this most exalted mood,
    With Arnstein and with Shirley I was sent
Upon a mission by the Brotherhood.
    Long afterward, I learned the full intent
Of that strange mission. Shirley understood
    Fully, and from the first, wherefore we went.
We traveled into Asia; here and there
Stopping,—for *what*, I did not know nor care.

XXV.

The wondrous East awoke unwonted awe
    In my young mind, and other things to me
Were nothing; though unusual signs I saw
    In my companions, of some mystery.
But in our Brotherhood there was a law
    Requiring neophytes to hear and see
Nothing, where his superiors were concerned:
Silence was the first lesson that we learned.

XXVI.

At that time, I was but a neophyte:
    Arnstein was older, and by many a grade
Higher in office; but our leader quite
    Threw Arnstein and all others into shade.
Shirley was now so powerful, he might
    Be called the right-hand of the Order's Head;
Without apparent effort he controlled
All who were thrown with him, both young and old.

XXVII.

In truth, despite our "free-and-equal" creed,
    There were degrees in our fraternal band:
No autocrat is more supreme, indeed,
    Than was the unknown Leader in command
Of this Free Order; nor could power exceed
    That wielded by the invisible Chief, whose hand
Directed all our movements, great or small:
Known but to few, his power was felt by all.

XXVIII.

Within this order, at its very core,
    There was another, wheel within a wheel;
A truly secret band, of which no more
    Was known, than that *it was*. Since *to reveal*
Was not more criminal than *to explore*
    The mysteries our leaders would conceal,
This inner power was known to very few,
And these but guessed, nor half believed it true.

XXIX.

And yet this inner-order was the pith,
    The very heart of our society,
Though generally regarded as a myth,
    Even by the few who guessed that it *might* be:
An unshorn Samson, neither cord nor withe
    Could bind this monster, safe in secrecy.
Its influence spread from land to land, by stealth—
Like a slow poison, undermining health.

XXX.

Nothing of this I dreamed, for, at the first,
    I was a dupe, one in a blind-led host
Of self-made victims; and their creed accurst
    I thought divine,—it was my pride and boast:
For I had *that* which makes men best or worst—
    Unflinching Faith, which never counts the cost.
Not easy of belief, a creed received
Clung to my mind as soul to body cleaved.

XXXI.

Shirley was one of the superior few
    Forming this subtle and mysterious ring
That swayed at will the uninitiate crew,
    The great majority who owned no king,
Nor law, nor God; enthusiasts, who nor knew
    Nor dreamed the Brotherhood was anything
But a great power for making all men free,
And leveling things to strict equality

XXXII.

We reached, in our erratic pilgrimage,
    Damascus, and for some time there remained.
There were so many objects to engage
    Attention, that awhile I well retained
My curious interest in a certain sage
    Called Selim of Damascus, who had gained
More wisdom than all men, alive or dead,
Save Solomon, himself: so rumor said.

XXXIII.

My comrades bade me not to seek this man,
    Though daily at his house they visited.
Arnstein grew melancholy, and began
    To elude my questions, with such signs of dread,
That my roused curiosity out-ran
    Discretion; and to Shirley thus I said:
"This great magician I demand to see,
This Solomon of the Nineteenth Century."

XXXIV.

Shirley upon me fixed his glowing eye,
    That seldom failed to conquer or to hold
The object of its solemn scrutiny.
    "Be not," he said, "so reckless or so bold;
For to his presence you will soon draw nigh,
    Above whose head a hundred years have rolled.
This very day it was arranged, indeed,
That you into his presence I should lead,—"

XXXV.

Here I broke in, half angry, half in sport:
    "'Lead me into his presence!' On my word,
'Tis Solomon, indeed, with all his court!"
    My scoffing jarred upon some tender chord,
For Shirley's eyes flashed fire, and, turning short,
    "Audacious!" he began,—when we both heard
A voice, as of some spirit in the air,
Low, soft, and most unearthly sweet—"*Beware!*"

XXXVI.

Amazed I stood, and like a coward shook,
    And fear, the most ungovernable thrilled
My very heart. Although the placid look
    Of Shirley now returned, his fingers chilled
With deadly cold my hand, which straight he took,
    And kindly said: "By this I know *'tis willed*
That you become initiate to-day:
May the Star shed on you his mildest ray!"

XXXVII.

I yielded, for my very soul was numb
    With some strange influence, *what*, I do not know;
And, led as one grown sightless, deaf, and dumb,
    Silent I walked between the silent two:
For Arnstein at our leader's call had come,
    Eager to see the neophyte go through
The initiation which had power to shake
His iron frame, as breezes move the brake.

XXXVIII.

The sage's house, like many another one
    In that old city, had an outer wall,
And courts inclosed but open to the sun,
    And many a gallery, and dim, cool hall.
The doors were open to our steps, but none
    Appeared to welcome us; deserted, all!
But for the lulling sound and silver gleam
Of playing fountains, silent as a dream.

XXXIX.

Through many still apartments I was led,
    Until we reached a door, where watching stood
A negro boy, most lightly garmented
    In tunic of fine silk as red as blood.
Except a crimson cap upon his head,
    And the silk tunic, he was wholly nude;
Jet-black, an ebon statue; lithe and tall,
With rounded limbs and shape symmetrical.

XL.

This negro fixed his bright black eyes on me,
    And, in good English—"Welcome, sir!" he cried.
He struck the door; a burst of melody
    Arose mysteriously, and failed, and died:
The door unclosed: behind it, we could see
    Rich hangings; which were lightly swept aside,
And Selim stood before us. Every one
Knelt down, as to a despot on his throne:

XLI.

All but myself. Shirley, the high and proud,
    The hard, cool Arnstein, and the page, knelt there;
All, prostrate in devotion, meekly bowed
    As Christians they derided kneel in prayer.
"Arise, my sons!" said Selim; clear, not loud,
    And sweet exceedingly his accents were.
He, too, spoke English, and the homely sound
Through the pleased ear into my spirit wound.

XLII.

Why he dwelt in Damascus, why the name
   Of Selim, I could not, and cannot tell:
His true name was not known, nor whence he came.
   Both hair and beard in waves of silver fell,
And crimson garments draped his stately frame,
   Suiting his regal mien and motions well.
Beneath the snowy eye-brows, light-grey eyes
Sparkled like keen, cold stars in winter skies.

XLIII.

His staff, surmounted by a silver ball,
   Was glittering-smooth and black as ebony;
About his head an oak-leaf coronal,
   Twined with green mistletoe, most strange to see!
As if a Druid in that Eastern hall
   Had risen to some spell of gramarye:
Such was my passing fancy—and I caught
The sage's eye, as though he read my thought.

XLIV.

"My son," he said, "all countries are my own
   All ages, future, present, past, are mine;
I represent all that the earth has known
   Of wisdom, art, and mystery divine.
A stronger seal than that of Solomon
   Shall press thy forehead with its mystic sign.
Young neophyte! this hand, which you behold,
The veil of Isis drew, in days of old!

XLV.

"Kneel! that the mystic seal may press thy brow."
    "Rash ingrate, kneel!" cried my companions each.
To whom I answered: "I have ceased to bow,
    Even to my father's God. And ye, who teach
Hatred to gods and tyrants—do you now
    Adore a mortal? Never act or speech
Of worship my free manhood shall degrade!
I serve no idols human thought has made."

XLVI.

"Calvert!" cried Shirley, in a voice that pained
    My heart with its deep tone of agony;
"Calvert! one hour has all too quickly waned,—
    O let no more such precious moments flee!
Never, while ages roll, can be regained,
    Once lost, this priceless opportunity.
Kneel! We will bow with you, and all engage
In homage to the justly-angered sage."

XLVII.

Raising my figure to its hight, I stood,
    Saying: "Kneel when it pleases you, and where!
But you seek freedom by the strangest road
    That ever led to bondage unaware.
I fear no mortal, and I serve no God:
    To none will I prefer a faithless prayer!"
So speaking, while deep anger swelled my heart,
And baffled hope, I turned me to depart.

XLVIII.

"Tarry, my son!" said Selim: Sweet the sound,
    Gifted with magic softness that low tone;
About my heart the sweet, strange accents wound,
    Holding me still when I would fain have gone.
"'Tis true, young man, that every soul has found
    An idol for its worship: you alone,
Sublime and self sufficient, dare avow
You serve no God, nor to a mortal bow.

XLIX.

"But go not hence in the belief that I,
    The old man Selim, was adored by these.
I am the high-priest of their deity—
    (I use these terms, that you with greater ease
May grasp my meaning).—See this mirror high!
    Its shadow-pictures vary as I please:
Look, thou, and learn! For in its depth shall glow
The shadow-types of gods to which ye bow!

L.

"The god of any man is what he loves;
    The ruling passion, which doth shape and mold
His character, and all his nature moves.
    But, see, the shadows from the glass have rolled—
Lo! Arnstein's god."
               As one whom it behooves
    Neither to be too timid nor too bold,
Arnstein approached with quiet dignity,
    Belied by pallid cheek and eager eye.

LI.

Upon the mirror's bright expanse was shown
    A picture most grotesque and mystical:
Arnstein's phantasm sat on a lofty throne,
    While pigmy human shapes before him fall,
Or dance, or strut, or swagger: he alone,
    Holding the strings that moved the puppets all.
Keenly observing them, he pulled the strings,
Experimenting on the pigmy things:

LII.

Much as a naturalist might scrutinize
    His captive beetles—with deep interest,
But nothing of affection in his eyes,
    Far less of fellow-feeling in his breast.—
"Is *Self* the god to whom I sacrifice?"
    Cried Arnstein; and his flushing face expressed
No anger, but astonishment and shame.
In Selim's softest tones the answer came.

LIII.

"It is a grand desire, my son, to rule
    By intellect,—your one desire is this;
A wish intense, that fills your spirit full;
    To gain it, is your highest dream of bliss:
For this, you make humanity your school;
    This sole, intense desire your idol is,
In serving which, you serve and bow before
The one great Master whom we all adore."

LIV.

Sudden, the crowned phantasm disappeared,
   With all its puppets. On the mirror's face
An inner room of some old temple reared
   Its arched and vaulted roof in shadowy space,
Wherein Egyptian Isis was revered;
   For there her veilèd shrine held solemn place,
And there, with upward face enrapt and pale,
Shirley's eidolon knelt before the Veil.

LV.

"My son," said Selim, turning then to me,
   "Would you not see the idol *you* revere?"
To whom I answered boldly: "I am free!
   I have no god.—" Then to the mirror clear
He spoke: "The god of his idolatry
   Let now upon your smooth expanse appear!"
Straightway, the temple vanished,—and there stood
A woman, with bare feet all bathed in blood,

LVI.

As she had walked upon a battle-field,
   Or on a scaffold where much blood was shed.
On her left arm she bore a brazen shield;
   Her foot was planted on a monarch's head,
And in her gory right hand did she wield
   A lance with cruel point all bloody-red;
A scarlet cap she wore, a flaming tiar
That crowned her streaming tresses as with fire.

LVII.

I knew this "goddess"—ay, her very name
    I had adored, almost from infancy;
And, strange to say, I felt no sense of shame,
    Though forced to see my own idolatry:
I thought it was a grand thing to proclaim
    My bondage as the slave of Liberty.
I knelt—and Selim stamped upon my brow
That broad and burning seal: I feel it now!

LVIII.

The sage's voice aroused me, clear and sweet:
    "Arise, my son! Nor measure by the past
Thy future life, with every joy replete,—
    Arnstein, go you with Addo, and in haste
Perform the task assigned. I will retreat
    With Shirley and this youth—our own, at last!"
He drew aside the hangings, and we three
Entered that room of triple secrecy.

LIX.

Your studio and that Oriental room
    Are not unlike: each is an octagon,
Each has a ceiling-casement to illume
    Walls windowless, with curtains flowing down;
And both are brightened by the lavish bloom
    Of many-colored garlands, winding on
From wall to wall, rich as a woodland bower
Built for a fairy in her sleeping-hour.

LX.

But, though the rooms are like on a first view,
    Yet, in particulars they differ much.
The window here is white, but *that* was blue,
    Faint, silvery; whitening with its pallid touch
All objects to a weird, unearthly hue:
    Not having seen, you scarce could fancy such.
The flowers upon *your* walls are painted there,
But *those* were living vines, trained thus with care.

LXI.

The fleecy curtains, whose white beauty fell
    Adown the flowery walls at intervals,
Each shaded, not a picture but a cell,
    Or niched recess, thus sunken in the walls.
What every niche contained I could not tell;
    Some were concealed behind voluminous falls
Of filmy lace, while others half disclose
Cushions and pillows fitting for repose.

LXII.

A living fountain in the center threw
    High in the air a double jet of spray—
Spray feathery-fine as mist, and clear as dew,
    Shining like hoar-frost in the morning's ray.
These jets, that made the sacred number *two*,
    Kept fresh a wreath that round the fountain lay,
A gorgeous garland, thick and long, where shone
The richest blossoms of the central zone.

LXIII.

The air was filled with perfumes, subtle, soft,
    And of a strange, intoxicating power;
An odor, as of musk and amber, oft
    Half-dizzied me: it came not from a flower,
(I thought), but from the jets that streamed aloft,
    Returning always in a feathery shower:
Come whence it might, so strong was this perfume,
It seemed to hang in clouds about the room.

LXIV.

They made me rest upon a silken heap
    Of cushions: Selim held to me a cup,
A marvelous shell, brought from the Indian deep,
    Holding rich wine; whereof I did but sup,
When both mine eyes grew dim with trancéd sleep:
    This partially passed off, and I looked up,
With senses supernaturally clear.
Yet wholly helpless, nor devoid of fear.

LXV.

I trembled: ringing noises in my head
    Hummed faintly as a distant swarm of bees:
Across mine eyes soft lights flashed rosy-red;
    Against each other smote my trembling knees,
Striving to stand: back on the cushioned bed
    I sank; and felt the creeping torpor freeze
My loathing heart, my vainly-struggling brain,
And glide with subtle speed through every vein.

LXVI.

Yet heard I Selim's accents—very low,
    But painfully distinct each measured tone:
"Shirley, take heed! this man will work us woe!
    He is not, and may never be, our own!"
Then Shirley's voice: "I will not let him go!
    Not for a world! He *shall* be ours alone!"
"Such strength of soul—of will," the sage replied,
"Is well worth winning to our Leader's side."

LXVII.

"McCartney is too light for such employ;
    But Arnstein and young Calvert I design,"
(Said Shirley's voice), "our agents to destroy
    The sceptered tyrants we have doomed. Be mine
The task to watch and to control this boy,
    Till by his agency we end the line
Of Northern autocrats: to Arnstein's hand
Be given the ruler of the Southern land."

LXVIII.

"My son! it were far better to allow
    The uninitiate to perform these deeds;
Be it an infidel who strikes the blow
    By which a system falls, a tyrant bleeds:
We worship the Light-bringing Star, who now
    Breaks through all clouds and on to glory leads:
The time approaches when both earth and sky
Shall fall before the Prince of Liberty!

LXIX.

"Then, free religion's sweet and simple rites
  Shall take the place of church and tyrant priest,
Who now all joy denies, all freedom blights:
  And when the oppressive system shall have ceased,
Then, Man shall know free Nature's full delights,
  And nations from their kings be all released
But Liberty's first step must be through blood—
Let not the initiate hand be thus imbrued.

LXX.

"We plan the work that should be done by those
  Who worship nothing—simple dupes of schools
They fathom not: nor will they dare disclose
  The secrets of the Order, whose strict rules
Doom treachery to death. Should freedom's foes
  Escape, and seize our agents—let the tools
And servants of the Order's outer-band
Be sacrificed—not those who understand.

LXXI.

"Beware of treason! Dark and strange to me
  The immediate future, veiled from my sight:
Nothing is clear as it was wont to be.
  That soul is struggling with immortal might!
Yes, he, the acknowledged slave of Liberty,
  Rebels against the source of Freedom's light!
Dread Powers against each other are arrayed:
Wait we—till there is call for human aid."

LXXII.

"Not so, my father!" Shirley's answer came.
 "Take off this charm, and leave him to my care!
Awake him *now*—and by that sacred flame,
 Our bright perpetual symbol, I will swear
This towering soul shall, like a falcon tame,
 Stoop to my call and join me anywhere!
Show him the plain, straight path to Liberty,—
He follows, though it leads through fire and sea!"

LXXIII.

"He walks the path that youthful dreamers tread,
 Bay-shadowed, and made soft by flowery sod:
Children with dreams and flatteries must be fed,—
 'Take of this fruit and thou shalt be a god!'
He eats—and lo, the path, indeed, is red,
 But not with flowers; his scepter is a rod!
This soul may be—nay, *will* be won, I trust,
But not by fruits of Eden, filled with dust.

LXXIV.

"This atheistic folly lasts not long,
 Nor untaught dreams of perfect Liberty,
In souls like his, so gentle, yet so strong:
 He had soon fallen to some idolatry,
As others have—some code of right and wrong;
 But, *now*, man's natural religion, free
As thought and wide as Nature, shall control
His spirit, and our Leader guide the whole."

LXXV.

"But, master," answered Shirley, hushed and low,
    In the still tone of hatred blent with awe;
"*There is a conflict?*"—"It is even so!"
    "May not the OTHER POWER, the Adverse Law,
May HE not conquer, to our overthrow?"—
    A third voice uttered one low word: "*Withdraw!*"
In gliding tones, so more than earthly sweet,
My torpid heart awoke and feebly beat.

LXXVI.

I was alone. Shirley had disappeared,
    And with him went the sage. I was alone.
The fountain's gentle rain was all I heard,
    Soothing me with its airy monotone.
My soul grew strong, and, like an untamed bird,
    Longed from its earthly prison to be gone,
Till all self-consciousness was lost, a change
Came o'er that mystic room, so startling-strange.

LXXVII.

The flowery room became a forest wide;
    The fountain slowly broadened to a lake;
The spray to misty clouds was magnified,
    Through which the moon seemed tenderly to break;
The gorgeous wreath that decked the fountain-side
    Changed to the semblance of a splendid snake,
A marvel of strange beauty: fold on fold
Gleaming with tints of emerald and gold;

LXXVIII.

With purple, glittering jet, and ruby flecked;
    With sapphire streaked, and glancing opal light:
The emerald of his lustrous throat was specked
    With spangling gold that sparkled starry-bright.
He reared on high his head, superbly decked
    With spherèd flame, that burned intensely white,
And, like a comet double-trained it sent
Two streams of light toward the firmament.

LXXIX.

The Serpent fixed his eyes on mine: no jewel
    Nor star shot ever such a potent ray;
So strong they seemed, yet nothing hard nor cruel,
    Moving my nature with resistless sway:
My spirit yielded to the soft subdual;
    Like music rose and fell my pulses' play,
Beneath the star-like darkness of the eyes,
Unfathomed depths of subtlest mysteries.

LXXX.

They were no serpent's eyes that drew me so;
    They held the light of immortality.
At times, with some unutterable woe,
    They gleamed and shifted like a troubled sea,
Until my own with grief would overflow:
    Then flashed the Serpent's eyes triumphantly,
Immortal beauty sparkling in their light,
Presaging deathless pleasures infinite.

LXXXI.

And still I gazed, while nearer crept the Snake,
    Till at my feet he stayed; and, fold on fold,
He laid himself in oval coils, to make
    A couch like that whereof the East has told,
When the drowned earth was liquid as a lake,
    For over her the shoreless ocean rolled:
So coiled the starry Snake, and richly shone
As jewels heaped to form an Eastern throne.

LXXXII.

Then, I, drawn onward by the powerful spell,
    Like Vishnu on the Serpent did recline;
And saw the lake, dilating, heave and swell,
    And lash the trembling shore with angry brine.
The forest fled—and deepest shadow fell,
    Illumined by the supernatural shine
Of the great star that crowned the Serpent's crest;
And we alone lived on the ocean's breast:

LXXXIII.

That vast and surging ocean, most appalling
    In its blank, borderless immensity.
I shrieked aloud in horror, wildly calling
    On the immortal Snake who carried me,
Lightly upon the billows rising, falling,
    The sole, the star-crowned sovereign of the sea:
" Ah, whither, mighty spirit! dost thou go?"
And straight the Serpent answered, soft and low;

LXXXIV.

In tones more gliding-smooth than music's own :
    "Fear nothing! I will bear thee o'er the tide.
Thou shalt learn mysteries to man unknown
    Since Egypt's knowledge from the earth has died!
Thou shalt behold a world long dead and gone;
    Ay, and the birth of thine own world beside :
And this, if thou but will it so, shall be
The first of many wonders thou shalt see.

LXXXV.

"Thou shalt be wiser than earth's wisest sage
    Since the fair planet was on nothing hung;
For thou thy thirst of knowledge shalt assuage
    With every drop of wisdom Time has wrung
From eons past—each wonder-working age
    Since time himself first into being sprung,
For to thy eager eyes will I unroll
The pages of a spirit-written scroll.

LXXXVI.

"But, first, I tell thee, (for thou couldst not see
    Nor understand those nameless mysteries
Coëval with unborn Eternity),
    That the great Origin of earth and skies
'In the beginning' made all things : for thee
    So much must, at the present time, suffice.
Then to the elements spake their Great Cause :
"LIGHT, BE!" her LORD commanded—and light was.

LXXXVII.

"Thou shalt first see the pre-Adamic earth,[4]
    The beautiful and starry child of light;
And thou shalt see the light that gave it birth,
    The stellar dust, whose living sparks unite
To form a glorious planet, better worth
    The loving care of the Eternal Might
Than ten such worlds as thine,—though never one
Now fairer makes its course around the sun.

LXXXVIII.

"The shade of elder earth shall now appear,
    A beauteous planet, long in ruins laid;
A mighty orb, as excellently clear
    As any star with glories yet to fade.
Ah, morning-star, light-bringer, whose full sphere
    In beauty and in glory was arrayed!
The home of those whose immortality
Thou couldst not share—nor could they die with thee!"

LXXXIX.

That wide, wild sea stretched far on every side,
    Its vast expanse in distant darkness lost;
It was so unimaginably wide
    That human thought its bounds could not have crossed;
But, now, in the dim distance, I descried
    A rising mist, pale as a glimmering ghost,
Start from the sea: warmer, and yet more warm
It grew—a nebulous cloud without a form:

XC.

A cloud that ever round its center curled,
    Still wheeling, changing, circling, resting not,
Till it took spheric shape, and ceaseless whirled
    With dizzying speed around the central spot,
Until a new-born star, a perfect world,
    Was thus from darkness and from chaos brought:
Then, for a space, its glory was withdrawn
Behind the gathering clouds that veiled its dawn.

XCI.

Soon, I beheld.—I will not madly seek
    That unimagined planet to portray,
Though like our earth, with sea and mountain-peak,
    And blissful valleys that between them lay;
Yet human language is too poor and weak
    To paint our own sweet world, far less array
That planet in its robe of beauty, worn
When first it rose, the fairest star of morn.

XCII.

Inhabitants it had, sublimer far
    Than pencil uninspired could hope to paint;
Shapes of ethereal beauty, such as are
    The visions of enraptured seer or saint;
Spirits enrobed in splendor, like a star,
    Divinely fair, and spotless of all taint;
Light is no clearer than their claritude,
Perfectly pure, and beautiful, and good.

XCIII.

Blind grew mine eyes with such expressive light;
    And when I looked again, there seemed to be
Some sinister and subtle change: less bright
    The planet shone, while over land and sea
A shadow crept, as of impending night:
    Discordant sounds were in the melody
That still arose.——Scarce was the planet seen,
So thick, so fast the shadow grew between

XCIV.

Still darker and more dense the shadow grew,
    With dusky wings outspread and covering all.
Lost was the lovely planet to the view,
    Shrouded as with an everlasting pall;
Till naught was there except the awful hue
    Of rolling darkness, gathered like a ball—
As black as if the darkness of despair
And woe unutterable hovered there.

XCV.

Again the Serpent's voice was at mine ear:
    "This shadow is a type. I cannot show
The cause of this dire change, nor make appear
    The fullness of this never-uttered woe.
It is not for a mortal ear to hear,
    Nor eye perceive, nor finite spirit know.
Already quails *thy* spirit, overcast
By the mere shadow of this long-dead Past."

XCVI.

Even as he spoke, there came a direful sound,
    A crash, a roar—as if that moment rent
A world from her foundations, and unbound
    Her elements, in wild confusion blent:
Space trembled, and the planets in their round
    Grew pale, as far and wide the horror went.
That sound swept by me like the voice of hell—
And into nothingness my spirit fell.

XCVII.

The soul-enticing accents of the Snake
    Aroused me from that deep and dizzy swoon:
"Too-fragile spirit, from thy trance awake!
    Thou shalt behold thine own fair world full soon
Her place among the starry myriads take,
    Linked to a sister-world, the mystic moon."
I looked, and saw the world so fair of late
All dark and desolate and devastate.

XCVIII.

Then said the Serpent: "These are shadows, all.
    There is no symbol for the Voice Divine,
Which from chaotic ruin did recall
    Order and beauty, till that earth of thine,
(As fair and good as that thou sawest fall,
    Though far less mighty), rose to sing and shine
Among her radiant sisters of the morn,
The stars who sang for joy that earth was born."[5]

XCIX.

I looked. The brooding darkness fled, revealing
 The earth as she appeared on her fifth day,
Upon her axis wheeling, ever wheeling:
 And lovely was the interlacing play
Of light and shade o'er her green bosom stealing,
 And soft her sister-planet's silver ray,
While sweet, unbidden harmonies unite
From both, as colors blend in purest white.

C.

Along the hills, with azure beauty crowned,
 Far-glancing streams, like veins of light, were seen;
A thousand rills and rivers glittering wound
 Through flowery vales of never-dying green,
Still flowing, flowing with harmonious sound
 To meet the seas that tossed in purple sheen
Their never-resting waves, that, shining, sang
To the great Source of light from whom they sprang.

CI.

There was no lack of living creatures, fair
 As their bright world: in myriad shapes, the seas
They filled with rainbow beauty, and the air
 Vibrated to aërial harmonies,
And to the countless wings sustaining there
 Bright birds that moved to their own melodies;
While roamed at will, upon the fragrant land,
Unnumbered creatures, beautiful and grand.

CII.

For the young earth was excellently fair,
    Adorned with every grace and every good.
There rose from her a voice of praise and prayer,
    Though yet upon her vernal soil had stood
No form of man; and joy was everywhere.
    Then said the Snake: "Let it be nearer viewed.
The landscape spread before thy charméd sight
Is Paradise, the Garden of Delight."

CIII.

While yet the soft tones lingered in mine ear,
    My spirit shrank, with a sharp sense of pain;
A shadowy horror, mightier far than fear,
    That stung to life my trancéd heart and brain.
The Serpent's voice I could no longer hear,
    Yet strength was palsied, and I strove in vain
To break from that dark, overwhelming Dread,
That bound and held me helpless as the dead.

CIV.

Again, all things were nothingness to me:
    And then, as sudden as the lightning's stroke,
My spirit sprang to life, and I was free!
    As if some binding chain that moment broke:
Fiercely my pulses beat, and blindingly
    Mine eyes throbbed, as my brain once more awoke.
Alone in that strange room I stood again,
Spray-sprinkled by the fountain's misty rain.

C V.

Alone, for aught of human presence nigh:—
    Yet, near me shone a faint, angelic form,
Who fixed on me her mild and steadfast eye,
    Profoundly sad, reproachful, yet so warm
With mother-love! Up-pointing to the sky,
    The pale and silent shape, with lifted arm,
A moment stood, then faded from my view.
It was my mother's shade, I saw, I knew!

C V I.

I felt the truth through all my trembling soul :
    She, whom I left on earth, was now in heaven !
Some pitying saint had burst the Snake's control,
    And light to the lost soul once more was given.

As the pure spirit passed, there softly stole
    Through the dusk room, a sound like rain at even,—
Thrice-mournful sounds, that grew till all the air
Was full of low lamenting and despair.

C V I I.

The conscious air, with viewless beings filled, ·
    To sounds of weeping, sighing and lament,
And flitting wave of restless wings, was thrilled :
    And still the mourning spirits came and went,
Unseen, but heard and felt : the air was stilled,
    But the sad sounds their mournful music blent,

While spirit-tones, of heavenly purity
And sweetness, spoke in question and reply:

First Voice.
Why mourn ye so?

Second Voice.
              For human woe,
  For a deeply-erring soul!
We weep for human sin and woe;
  For days of dread that nearer roll,
When fire shall glow, and blood shall flow,
And the good, and the bad, and the high and the low
Shall weep, nor any comfort know;
Shall mourn—as we for coming woe
  In the days of death and dole!

First Voice.
And will the Lord of Worlds leave one so fair
To perish in her sin and her despair?
The turbulent, ungoverned multitude
Have cast God's altars down—yet has not He
His people, who have never bowed the knee
To the world's god of anarchy and blood?
Will he forsake the nations utterly?

Second Voice.
They drink the poisoned draught themselves distilled;
They walk the chosen way their hearts have willed,

The doomed and downward way forever trod
By all the nations who forget their God!

First Voice.

And must the heavy curse so surely fall?

Second Voice.

Near and more near the days of ruin crawl,
Like lapping waves that undermine a wall,
      Till they shall overflow,
And sweep the desolated world with woe!

End of Part First.

NOTES TO THE LIGHT-BRINGER.

PROEM.

1. I. "*The house of Silverlinn was large and tall.*"

The description of this country-seat is not overdrawn. The real residence which suggested the imaginary Silverlinn had a terraced garden containing *an acre* of hyacinths, of which plant the owner was very fond.

2. XXX. "*Bright as the Indian Cupid.*"

The *East* Indian Cupid,—he who floated down the Ganges on a blue lotus.

CANTO I.

1. V. "*Shaksperc.*"

Thus the poet most frequently spelled his own name, and (in the writer's opinion) it is preferable to the modern *Shakspeare*. At all events, where the orthography is disputed, each admirer of the great poet may choose his own way of spelling the revered name.

2. VII. "*To him the Prophet's woe did well belong.*"

"Woe unto them that call evil good, and good evil; that put darkness for light, and light for darkness; that put bitter for sweet, and sweet for bitter."—*Isaiah ch.* v; *v.* 20.

It is not surprising that the unhappy poet, to whom this line refers,—whose genius was equaled, if not surpassed by his *anti-morality*—should be admired and praised by the atheistic or the irreligious part of humanity; but when professed Christians defend, and "eminent" clergymen eulogize him, the spectacle is simply astounding.

3. XIV. "*He welcomed Darwin's theory.*"

The author, who knows nothing of "Darwin's theory," must not be understood as asserting that this philosopher does (or does not) believe in the existence of the soul: the words given to the imaginary *McCartney* are those of a professed follower of Darwin—but the disciples of modern philosophers do not always comprehend their meaning.

4. LXXXVII. "*Thou shalt first see the pre-Adamic earth.*"
This is the *Serpent* speaking; not the author.

5. XCVIII. "*For joy that earth was born.*"

This theory, that the planet we inhabit was made of the fragments of a former world, is old and well known: but it must not be supposed the writer's belief. The *Serpent*, as the agent of the Evil Principle, would subtly re-echo the youth's own speculations; and present skeptical ideas to him in the most seductive and even semi-religious light. For, those who know least of poor humanity cannot fail to see, if they observe at all, that the great Tempter varies his modes of attack to suit every soul: of late days, frequently taking the guise of "honest doubt," "inquiry after truth," etc.; the temptation to which all thinking souls seem (in these "perilous times") to be subjected, at some period of life.

MARCELLA:

A ROMANCE OF THE BLUE RIDGE.

Whoever comes to shroud me, do not harm,
   Nor question much,
This subtile wreath of hair about mine arm—
   The mystery, the sign, thou must not touch.
                              —CRASHAW.

INTRODUCTION.

I.

In eighteen-hundred-seventy-six—the year
To Freedom and America so dear—
A lady died, at Florence, in the prime
Of spring, and of her own life's summer-time.

They called her "gentle stranger;" "kind unknown;"
She was a widow, rich, but quite alone.
Society she shunned, but to her door
Came daily throngs of hungry, half-clad poor.
Freely, unquestioning, her aid was given
To just and unjust, like the rains of heaven.
Alone the lady lived, and lonely died.

II.

Those who arrayed her for the grave descried
A closely-fitting sleeve of cloth-of-gold—
So first it seemed—about the left arm rolled;
But, when they looked more narrowly, they found
It was a long and curious bracelet, wound
In spiral bands, and woven of bright hair,
The gold threads stained and darkened, here and there,

As if it had been dipped in blood.   This charm
From wrist to shoulder covered the whole arm.
It seemed impossible that hair could be
Of such bright length and silken quality ;·
Most strange—yet so it was.
       They left it there,
Twined round the arm, that cherished wreath of hair,
And when the lady in her tomb was laid,
They buried with her there the golden braid.

III.

But, what, then, was her story ?   Who was she,
Who that strange token wore so secretly ?
American by birth.   Upon the stone
Above her foreign grave, her name alone—
ADELAIDE LOVELACE — was inscribed.   No more
It told to strangers than they knew before
Of her, who, wrapped in sorrow or in pride,
Alone had lived, alone at Florence died.

CANTO I.

I.

Our "Old Dominion," in her palmy day,
Could many a stately mansion-house display
Fair as Park Aubray, where our scene is laid:
Some yet remain, neglected and decayed,
Or, having passed to strangers, are bedecked
In new "improvements," worse then all neglect;
But some are lovely still, through change and chance
Of time, and war, and adverse circumstance.
Park Aubray, beautiful and lonely, stands
Deserted, in a waste of lonely lands;
For brave must be the tenant who would dare
To dwell within the mansion moldering there,
To all the country-side a place of dread,
A "haunted house," the dwelling of the dead.

The present owner, though of Aubray blood,
Beneath its moss-grown roof has never stood.
A distant kinsman, being the heir-at-law,
Owns Aubray Park, a place he never saw.
By will, he was the chosen heir, beside,
Of her who recently at Florence died,

Adelaide Lovelace—of the Aubray race
The last who owned the Aubray dwelling-place,
Ere the estate to this new master passed,
Who left it what he found, a lonely waste;
For he is one of those who, having lost
The "Cause" they fought for, cling to its "poor ghost."
Self-exiled from his native land, he strays
From realm to realm, and dreams thro' aimless days.

II.

So, Aubray Park stands lonely; fortunate,
Despite misfortune. Better such a fate—
Better in lonely grandeur to decay,
Than have its silvan beauty swept away
By paint and "progress," till its time-won grace
And Old-World quaintness vanish from the place.
And, though its rightful owners come no more,
At least, no stranger-lord has crossed its door;
The great, wide mirrors in the drawing-room
Still glimmer palely through the silent gloom,
Reflect the portraits on the dusty wall,
Brave men, fair women—fading shadows, all!
But on those mirrors, no strange master's face
Even for a fleeting moment has found place;
In the old library no stranger-hand
Has touched the books—nor careless eye hath scanned
Time-honored manuscripts and volumes worn,
That, like their owners, will to dust return—

And a young poet's songs, whose every word
Came music-laden as a mocking-bird.
Those solitary halls and chambers mute
Give back no echo to the stranger's foot.

III.

"Park Aubray" was the sounding name bestowed
By Edmond d' Aubray on his loved abode,
New-built when he from England crossed the sea,
From Cromwell, the "Protector" forced to flee.
Virginia bent to the usurper's reign,
But Aubray dwelt unharmed on his domain.
The Restoration came; but he had grown
To love this new land, dearer than his own :
French by his parentage, though English-born,
The loss of England he had ceased to mourn;
Looked on the growing colony with pride,
And loved Park Aubray, where, in time, he died.

IV.

Built of red brick, the dark old mansion stood
On level land, surrounded by a wood,
A grove of Spanish oaks,[1] whose branches threw
An arch of green across the avenue.
Fine, closely-shaven grass grew in the shade,
And petted fawns in dappled beauty strayed,
Where the wild pheasant's plumes of spotted gold,
And crested peacocks' starry trains unfold.
One sunny spot there was : a space before

The stone steps leading to the great hall door,
Was full of richest flowers: a fairy view
Down the long vista of the avenue.
Elsewhere, upon the green that swept away
Throughout the grove, no shrub nor blossom gay
A human hand had set; yet all in flower
The oak-grove blazed: each tree was one great bower
Of trumpet-vines, that clothed from branch to root
The trees in one rich mass of leaf and shoot
And crimson bloom. The gorgeous parasites
Climbed to the boughs and wreathed the topmost heights.
Long years, the trees bore up their blooming foes,
And still the bell-flower by the acorn grows;
The stately trees no loss of strength betray
Under the vines would draw their life away,
But robed and crowned, stand as they long have stood,
Like the strange growth of some enchanted wood.

V.

Old Mrs. Lovelace long had owned this place,
In eighteen-thirty-eight. Of Aubray race
Was she; a race self-willed, high-hearted, proud;
With strength of mind and beauty well endowed.
Some vices, many virtues they could show;
Forgot no friend, but could forgive a foe:
And foes they had, as all must have: though few
The friends they sought, seldom were these untrue.
Love is the recompense of love, 'tis said,
And one great virtue these proud Aubrays had,

A virtue few possess, but all approve—
Fidelity in friendship or in love.
His word, once pledged, no Aubray ever broke,
Nor trust betrayed, nor any friend forsook,
But held, through good and ill, his steadfast faith,
Till the great, loving heart was stilled in death.
But, once betrayed, an Aubray's trusting heart
Knew naught of patient faith, the nobler part:
Like the famed crystal, said to break in twain
At touch of poison, so, at falsehood's stain
His love, his faith, his trust, in fragments broke,
And all the savage in his nature woke.

VI.

And Helen Lovelace was (as has been said)
An Aubray born. Her husband, long since dead,
Had left no children, so the lady sought
Heirs among her own relatives, and brought
To Aubray Park her brother's widowed bride;
But, in the self-same year, she, also, died,
Leaving an infant daughter, fair of face—
The youngest blossom of the Aubray race.
Nourished by her fond aunt with tender care,
The lovely infant grew to childhood fair,
So fair that she deserved her name of Blanche:
White as a May-bloom on a bending branch,
Or summer cloudlet in a sky of blue,
To peerless maidenhood Blanche Aubray grew.

VII.

But Helen Lovelace had another niece,
Her sister's child: the mother's late decease
In a far distant State, her child had thrown
Friendless upon the world, helpless, and lone.
Adelaide Aubray, in the days long past,
Had made a love-match little to the taste
Of her proud kindred, with a Northern youth,
And, for his sake, had left her native South.
Young love against old blood but lightly weighed:
The only dower given to Adelaide
Was bitter anger, or more cruel scorn,
Or cold contempt. Had he been gentle-born,
Had he their equal seemed to Aubray eyes,
This story might have ended otherwise.
His poverty, indeed, was not a sin
In well-born Southern eyes, but Herbert Linn
Nor had, nor honored, claims to gentle blood:
From points opposing, each the subject viewed,
Linn thinking it enough to be a man
Cultured and true, a good republican;
But the proud race with which he was allied
Were born and bred aristocrats, whose pride
Was far above all thought of golden gain,
And low-born culture eyed with calm disdain:[2]
Linn wanted all things, measured by their rule—
A low-born Yankee youth, who "kept a school."

So, "all for love," the haughty Aubray belle
Wedded, and lost her world. If it were "well"
For her, I know not, nor for him she loved.
To the far North the youthful pair removed,
And, after years of hopeless poverty,
The husband died, and Adelaide was free
To seek, if so she willed, her Southern home.
They would have welcomed her if she had come,
But of her husband's death they had not heard,
For Adelaide nor wrote nor sent a word
To her proud kindred, but, from year to year
Remained as lost to them as they to her.
Her husband's relatives were poor enough,
But helped her as they could: her life was rough
And hard; but armed in pride and love's own strength,
She fought life's battle well; and when, at length,
She yielded,—t'was to that all-conquering one
None can resist—she bowed to death alone:
Then, from her death-bed to her sister sent,
Asking, if Aubray pride would yet relent?
Not for herself she sought their tardy aid,
But for her child, the younger Adelaide.
Before her message reached them she was dead.
Not through green meadows did her life-path lead,
Nor by still waters: few and evil were
Her days, and welcome was the grave to her.

VIII.

And thus to Aubray Park came Adelaide Linn,
A charming girl as ever smiled therein.
To both these orphan girls their kind aunt strove
Due care to give, and full, impartial love;
But Blanche was still, in truth, the favorite child:
Adelaide's manners were more smooth and mild,
But the bright, mischief-loving Blanche had been
From baby-hood Park Aubray's fairy queen,
Beloved by all her subjects, black and white.
She was the Aubray heiress, too, by right:
Her grandsire, in his later days, had meant
Park Aubray for his son: but this intent
Untimely death forbade him to fulfill.
His elder daughter knew her father's will,
And, as the old man wished it, even so,
(She said), to Blanche the Aubray land should go.

IX.

And never was a mocking-bird more wild,
More free and joyous, than this lovely child.
Incarnate joy she seemed, and in her glee
Fearless and frank as innocence can be;
Loving and trusting as those are who know
Their own hearts faithful, and deem others so.
Blanche was an Aubray: many traits she had
Of Aubray character, both good and bad;
But Adelaide showed not, in mind or face,
The slightest kindred to her mother's race.

Alien alike in feature and in soul,
Gifted with patience and with self-control,
Gentle of look—to Aubray Park she came,
Trained all her life to hate the Aubray name.

X.

But beauty's charm was hers: a woven crown
Of wreathed and braided tresses, chesnut-brown,
Adorned her graceful head, and waved across
The low, white brow in satin-shining gloss.
The downward eyes half hid their violet light
Beneath white lids and lashes golden-bright:
Arbutus-bells are not more pinky-pure
Than her smooth cheek and maiden mouth demure,
And her sweet voice was always soft and low—
"An excellent thing in woman," as we know.

Like two fond sisters, Blanche and Adelaide
Together rode, and walked, and sung, and played,
Studied, and sewed, or practiced household arts
With equal minds and undivided hearts.

XI.

Five years passed quickly, thus. Blanche was eighteen,
And Adelaide some twenty years had seen,
When rumor whispered—and the whisper flew—
Of trouble at the Park. The rumor grew,
And gathered strength, like fire from some faint spark:
"Great trouble had arisen at Aubray Park."

One of the girls so deeply loved, and bred
As daughters of the house, dark rumor said,
Had, snake-like, stung the hand they should have kissed:
One of them was—*an abolitionist!*

An abolitionist![3]   And was *this* all?
It was enough, at least. Of words that fall
With most of utter horror in their tone,
Of hatred and abhorence, there was none
That smote like this upon a Southron's ear;
It brought a thrill of loathing, scorn, and fear,
As one who, walking with incautious tread,
Sees in his path a lurking copperhead.

By the term "abolitionist," they meant
A secret foe, whose merciless intent
Was, to incite the slaves—an untaught host—
To insurrection, reckless of the cost.
Yet, there were Southrons who did not believe
The "right-divine" of slavery, nor receive
With faith unquestioning the creed that gave
Freedom to them and bondage to the slave;
But, he who hated slavery, loathed yet more
The spy-conspirator, whose subtle power
Kept him forever trembling lest the torch
Be first applied to his own vine-wreathed porch.

XII.

A servile insurrection, who can paint?
When, crazed with sudden, boundless unrestraint,

Slaves revel in the drunkenness of blood;
And all alike, the guilty and the good,
Share the same doom; and youth and age expire,
And the whole land is red with blood and fire.

That the unpitied Southrons did not know
The fullness of this unexampled woe,
They thank the slave: content to bide his time,
His patient shrewdness did not stoop to crime;
Whether through prudence or through gentleness,
Grateful remembrance is his due no less:
The slave struck, if at all, in open strife,
Nor won his freedom by the assassin's knife.

XIII.

And one of Aubray race had now become
A traitor to her country, State, and home;
"Caught by the abolition fantasy,
Of wholesale freedom and philanthropy:"
Such the most *charitable* view of one
Whom friends and kindred all agreed to shun,
Like a poor, plague-struck outcast:—dire disgrace
To one of those fair girls of Aubray race!

Which one? Of course the Northern Adelaide,
Triumphant rumor said—then stopped, dismayed.
Like a bright blossom from a wind-blown tree,
Or silver rain-drop on a stormy sea,

So sweet Blanche Aubray from her station fell.
She vanished—how or whither, none could tell;
But this was certain,—she had disappeared
From Aubray Park, the home where she was reared.

XIV.

And none to Mrs. Lovelace dared to break
The silence she imposed; none dared to speak
Aloud the graceful name once so beloved.
Blanche Aubray's portrait was at once removed,
No one knew whither; but a tale went round
Of hidden rooms and cellars underground
At Aubray, and, in these, the gossips held,
The portrait and the girl were both concealed.
But time went on, unmoved; and day by day,
These idle rumors, fading, passed away.

Adelaide Linn now held unbounded sway
At Aubray Park; and when her kind aunt died
In the same year, (of wounded love and pride,
Not less than age), she left the Aubray land,
And all the fortune at her own command,
To Adelaide; with only this request—
That she should wed Charles Lovelace: this behest
Suited both Lovelace and fair Adelaide,
Nor was the auspicious marriage long delayed.

XV.

Charles Lovelace was her nephew by the tie
Of marriage merely: in the days gone by
He often came to Aubray, and had played
In childhood both with Blanche and Adelaide.
The wedding over, Helen Lovelace died,
Old, broken-hearted, crushed in hope and pride;
And in the willow-shaded burial-place
She slept, with many more of Aubray race.
Age fitly died, and youth as fitly reigned;
While, Blanche, forgotten as the dead, remained
Lost, as completely as a wandering star:
And then, in five more years, came civil war.

CANTO II.

I.

In eighteen-hundred-sixty-three, in days
When civil war had set the land a-blaze;
The days of martial deeds; the whirling time
Of tears and laughter, wild romance and crime;
Daring adventures; revels; wretchedness;
And some true hearts and patriot souls no less;
When anarchy seemed broken loose, at last,
And nothing in the "reeling world" stood fast;—
At Aubray Park occurred, in that strange time,
Events as wild as e'er were told in rhyme,
And tragic as the year from which they date—
Events that left Park Aubray desolate.

II.

Charles Lovelace, rousing at the first alarm
Of war, rushed to the conflict. Young and warm,
And Southern to the center of his heart,
He played in Southern cause a gallant part:
Meantime, his wife was left alone to wait
Her lord's return, in semi-widowed state.

Adelaide Lovelace, wealthy, fair and young,
Her charms the theme of every flattering tongue,
Gifted with wit, in grace beyond compare,
Seemed beauty's darling and good fortune's heir.
And, yet, her life was not all happiness;
Joy was not all those features could express:
Sometimes, when gayety was at its height,
Her head would droop, like flowers at sudden blight,
While on her glooming brow and darkened eye
Rested the shade of some sad memory:
And oft, for days, both face and manner wore
A brooding sadness never seen of yore.

'Twas said, that in the lady's charming home
Demons of doubt and jealousy found room ;
They said her lord's distrust made dark her life,
Too much a tyrant to his fair young wife.
That Lovelace worshiped her, was plain and clear;
As plain, that she regarded him with fear;
But love and fear might well be found combined
For one whose very tyranny was kind,
Arising from the love that would not brook
To lose one smile of hers, nor share one look.
She did not smile the more when he was gone,
Nor grew her brow less sad when left alone:
But those were wild and anxious times, at best,
And few could boast a spirit all at rest.

III.

On a still summer evening, Adelaide
Through the green park alone and thoughtful strayed.
Eastward the shadows sloped, and western light
Trembled across the mere[1] all rosy-bright.
Bathed in the radiance of the sunset glow,
Across the park she passed with footstep slow;
Tracing the pool along its winding bank,
Under the willows, growing rank by rank,
Until she reached the limit of the mere:
From the steep-sloping cliff, a streamlet clear,
Broke, ere it reached the darker pool below,
Into three rills, soft-tinkling as they go.
With spreading boughs, and "more than common tall,"
A holly grew beside the triple fall;
And, higher on the cliff, magnolias grew,
Azaleas, laurels, and wild ivy,[2] too;
Cresting the hill, great, solemn cedars stood,
Inmixed with pine—a dark and sombre wood.
Below the waterfall, beside the mere,
Which spread its waters dark but amber-clear,
A huge oak, rich in mistletoe and moss,
Cast its broad shadow half the pool across.
Beneath this shaggy oak, a large grey stone,
With lichens green and mosses overgrown,
Seemed rudely fashioned for a great arm-chair—
Fashioned by Nature's hand, who placed it there.
In pensive mood, the lady rested here,
Gazing with dreamy eyes upon the mere.

IV.

Was it the wind, that moving fitfully
Through the full foliage, sounded like a sigh?
Was it the water-fall's sweet monotone
Which her sad fancy turned into a moan?
Above the woodland odors, she can tell
The scent of crushed sweet-brake,[3] she knows it well;
And, once again, that soft, low breathing came,
In tremulous tones that uttered her own name.
Startled, she turns, and barely can discern
A crouching figure, hidden in the fern;
A pair of eyes that matched her own in hue,
And features that full well the lady knew.
Adelaide, with a faintly-uttered scream,
Sinks back upon the stone. As in a dream,
She sees the youth, who, kneeling at her feet,
Seems earnestly her pity to entreat.
It seemed a Southern soldier who thus lay,
Clad in a full suit of Confederate grey.

V.

Giddy as from a swoon, the lady gazed
Upon the features to her own up-raised:
It was a handsome face, worth looking on.
The rich blue eyes like living jewels shone,
And the short, curling locks of flaxen hair
Waved round a forehead femininely fair,
Shading a beardless cheek, more white, by far,
Than sun-touched cheeks of soldiers often are.

"Adelaide, dearest Adelaide!" she hears:
"By all the memories of our childhood's years,
By your own heart, and by your father's grave,
Pity your kinsman, and, in pitying save!"

VI.

"What do you here?" spoke faintly Adelaide;
And pressed with trembling hand the fallen braid
Back from her moistened brow and bloodless cheek.
"Tell me—but no! *This* is no time to speak—"

"Stay, but a moment! Some short space allow—"

"No, no! I cannot—dare not hear you now!
For in these tell-tale woodlands may be heard
Too far the wingéd echo of a word.
There is a pleasant grotto in this hill,
Where you may bide till nightfall, if you will.
'Tis fitted up a silvan reading-room,
And you may rest till twilight shadows come,
In safety; for, *there*, none will dare intrude
Upon your resting-place, secure, though rude."

"I know the place, for it was there I lay,
O'er-worn with toil, the morn of this long day."

"Thither return, and tarry for the shade
Of friendly night: 'twill not be long delayed,
For, see, the light has faded from the mere.
Adieu, till then. I may not linger here!

Trust to my love, Romaine! To profit you,
Nothing shall be undone that I can do!"

She clasped his hand—then turned, and thro' the dark
Of gathering shades, fled home across the park.

VII.

Reaching her own apartment, there she found
Her favorite maid, Marcella. Glancing round,
As to be sure no listener could be nigh—
"Marcella!" said her mistress: "you and I
Have dwelt together more like friend and friend
Than maid and mistress. Can I now depend
On your affection and fidelity?"
"Miss Adelaide, I've served you faithfully,"
Replied Marcella, "and will do so now.
It but remains for you to show me how."

"Do you remember," answered Adelaide,
"My cousin, who once here at Aubray stayed
A week or more? His name is Romaine Linn."
Marcella smiled. "One of your Northern kin,
Of whom our master is so jealous?"
                              "Yes;
And this remembrance adds to my distress.
Of Major Lovelace I could ask no aid,
Even were he here at home;" said Adelaide.
"More brother-like than cousin-like to me
Is Romaine, whom I loved from infancy.

He is my junior by six years, or more;
My pet and favorite in the days before
I came to Aubray Park. For many a year
With Romaine passed my childhood: not more dear
Can any brother to his sister be,
Than my young cousin, Romaine Linn, to me.
And he is in great peril! in disguise,
Hid in the grot of Cedar Hill he lies.
I know not whence he comes, nor why, nor how!
He held the rank of captain, *that* I know,
In our—I mean, the Northern army."
       "Why,"
Answered Marcella, "does he hidden lie
Within the Southern lines? *Is he a spy?*"

All trace of red the lady's cheek forsook;
Her very lips a death-like pallor took:
"*Silence!*" she breathed. Marcella drew more near,
And in low murmurs at her lady's ear,
Talked earnestly and long: and Adelaide
Grew calmer, as she listened to the maid.

VIII.

Of living creatures in the world beside,
The lady on this slave the most relied.
Marcella's story was a curious one:
An Aubray slave, she was not born upon

The domain of Park Aubray, but away
On a plantation that in lowlands lay,
Beside the river.   Ere she was full-grown
She fled from slavery, and it was known
That she reached Canada.   Years passed away,
When suddenly, one memorable day,
She re-appeared at Aubray.   Adelaide
At Aubray Park the "rod of empire" swayed
At this time, and to her Marcella went.
"She'd learned," she said, "to bitterly repent
Exchanging the light tasks of slavery
For ceaseless toils and perils of the free.
Would not Miss Adelaide forgive?   Once more
Try her, she'd be more faithful than before."
And Adelaide, pleased at the girl's return,
And at the lesson other slaves might learn
From this repentant fugitive,—forgave,
And, far from punishing the regained slave,
Placed her about her person; where full soon
The intelligent and beautiful quadroon
Gained Adelaide's full confidence.   And she,
Marcella, served her mistress faithfully,
As if she always and by all means strove
To prove her grateful and devoted love.

IX.

The hours, to Romaine on his cavern floor,
More slowly passed than e'er did hours before.

Weary was he, and hungry, sick, and cold;
He felt the chilly darkness round him fold,
And, almost swooning in his weakness, lay
Dreading yet longing for the coming day.
At last, he saw a shadow flit before
The glimmering half-light of the cavern door;
A light form bent, a quick foot stepped within,
And a low voice spoke softly: "Captain Linn?"

"Who is it? Not my cousin Adelaide?"

"No," said the low, sweet tones: "I am her maid."

She pressed a match against the cavern-side,
And the small jet of flame at once applied
To a light lamp she carried in her hand;
And by the steady beam she closely scanned
The features of the Northman: he surveyed
In turn, the features of the quadroon maid.
The lamp she held was raised above her head,
And a bright ring of light around her spread,
Revealing to Romaine's astonished gaze
A form of loveliness beyond all praise.
But, though she stood within a halo bright,
Yet had she neither saint's nor angel's light:
Rather, in baleful beauty threatening
As Lamia, from her coil about to spring,
Or wild enchantress in a magic ring.

X.

Not like a common slave was she arrayed;[4]
Her rich attire confessed the favorite maid.
Her flowing skirt was deepest violet-hue,
But the gay jacket shone in brightest blue,
With rows of silver buttons, silver braid,
And silver tassels, twinkling as they swayed.
About her head in full but graceful fold,
A silken sash of finest blue was rolled,
And where the ends with careless grace were tied,
They swept her shoulders with their fringes wide.
This turban hid the hair, except a row
Of short, black curls across her forehead low—
So low, the tiny ringlets almost met
The fine, straight eyebrow's line of perfect jet.
Upon her cheek's dark oval deeply glows
The dusky crimson of a velvet rose;
Her mouth betrays no sign of negro race—
Fine, faultless lips, a sculptor's dream of grace,
Somewhat too cold and stern, too closely shut,
And hard and red as if from coral cut.
The straight Greek nose a model might have been
For the proud profile of some captive queen;
The thin ·dilating nostril, though not wide,
Expanding easily with scorn or pride.
But, when she speaks, the parting lips reveal
A flash of teeth that sparkle like cut-steel—
Teeth whose metallic luster almost vies

With the hard brilliance of her deep black eyes;
And strange it was that human eyes could shine
With light so cold, with beauty so malign.
Their sharp, cold light is shaded and half hid
By the thick fringes of the half-closed lid,
But, even in deep repose, seems fraught with harm,
Like the sheathed lightnings of a rising storm.

XI.

But from those chiseled lips the voice that came
Might put the soul of melody to shame.
O sweetest tones! whose breathings clearer are
Than May-dew trembling to the morning star;
Softer than velvet, and as rich as musk
Or full-blown tuberose in the dewy dusk.

"My name, sir, is Marcella. I am here
Because my mistress cou d not come: we fear
Of other slaves the ready ear, quick eye,
And busy tongue, that lets no rumor die.
My mistress would inquire of you, through me,
Why you have hither come, so recklessly?
Young man, you wish to lose your life, 'tis plain."

"Not so; I wish to save it," said Romaine.
"At least, I would not die in such a way,
If I might choose. But, briefly, let me say:

XII.

"At the late forward movement made by Lee,
It happened (most unhappily for me),
That I had leave to visit on a farm
Not far from camp. My visit did no harm
To any but myself: with best intent
(Indeed, to aid some union friends) I went.
The enemy's advance was sudden: there
Was I, within his lines: my host, with fear
Beside himself, implored me, for *his* sake
And for his household, some disguise to take;
This suit, which now I wear, of Southern grey,
He begged me to assume, for but a day,
Till the Confederates should be gone—and then
He'd guide me to the Federal lines again.
Were I, a Yankee, found beneath his roof
As guest and friend, he said, it were enough
To ruin him and other friends beside:
And so, with his entreaties I complied,
(Weakly, indeed,) because I would not be
The ruin of the roof that sheltered me.

I faint with fasting and with pain. Not now
Can I relate to you where, when, and how,
I sought to pass the Southern lines—in vain!
Within the rebel lines I still remain,
And in disguise. If they should find me here,
I die—but death alone I do not fear,
For there are harder things, than just to die:

They hang me, if they take me, for a spy!
Go tell your lady this! 'Tis no disgrace
To say that *such* a death I dare not face!
But other means of death are in my reach,
And, if she cannot aid me—"
       "Spare your speech,"
Replied Marcella. "I am here to save.
Arise, and quit this cold and cheerless cave;
No safe asylum, this! Ere now, in truth,
You had been mangled by the watch-dog's tooth,
But I have bribed the keeper of the beast
To house him safely, for this night, at least."

Romaine spoke not, for faintness. The quadroon
Bent down and shook him lightly, "Do not swoon!
Rouse all your strength, at once, and come with me
Where you may rest in full security.
You shall have food, wine, everything you need:
Summon your strength, and follow me, with speed!"

XIII.

Extinguishing the lamp, that no least ray
Like glancing wildfire might their course betray,
She hastened from the cave; he followed fast
As weakness could: the winding mere once passed,
They crossed the park, and neared the mansion tall:
Marcella paused in shadow of the wall.
Romaine could now perceive they stood before
The yawning blackness of a cellar-door.

Descending here, the heavy air grew thick
With dampness, like a grave: his heart beat quick
With weakness and excitement, when, once more
Pausing, his guide unclosed a second door,
Whose hinges grated. Now the air, though damp,
Was stifling close. Marcella here the lamp
Relighted: in a narrow passage, there
Like a step-ladder, was a rude, steep stair,
Seen dimly in the gloom; up this they went:
The shaded lamp a feeble radiance lent,
Showing a straight, short landing; at the end,
Another flight of steps, which they ascend,
Reaching a longer passage, narrow, tall,
And thick with dust: their garments brushed the wall
On either side, as silently they passed,
Until they reached a third door, and the last.

XIV.

This door she opened. Light and soft perfume
Greet them on entering this small, secret room.
'Twas a mere closet; but no fairy hall
Were more inviting, than that chamber small.
The floor was covered with a matting fine,
Gold-hued, and brightened by a scarlet line;
The walls were paneled with a smooth, pale wood,
Which mellow time had now made amber-hued.
A crimson couch, with pillows snowy fair,
Woo'd to repose; and a great easy chair

Cushioned with crimson velvet, waiting stood
Beside a table heaped with dainty food:
Bread, in white puffs, like cotton; biscuits thin,
Light-brown without, but snowy-white within,
On tintless china. Pheasant broiled, and fish,
Each neatly placed upon a pearl-white dish;
Butter, both creamy-white and yellow-gold;
And dark-red jelly, quivering from the mold;
Snow-sugared cake, of fruits and spices full;
Pure honey, candied to an amber dull;
A great decanter of Bohemian glass;—
Through the transparent crystal interlace
Green vinings, branched and wreathed in quaint device,
Like river-mosses under new-made ice,—
This held rich juice of Carolina's vine,
The sun-ripe Scuppernong, the Southern wine:
In crystal bowls were fruits and berries set; —
Bowls veined with ruby and with violet;
And a rich cup of cream, to crown the feast,
So thick it fell in droplets; last, not least,
A silver urn held coffee clear as wine.
Gold-brown as amber, with aroma fine—
Had the Greek gods inhaled it, coffee then
Had been their drink, and nectar left for men.

XV.

"Here's food and wine and safety," said the slave.
"Whatever more is needed, you shall have.

To-morrow, if *I* do not visit you,
Some other surely will.   Till then, adieu."
She turned and left the room.   Romaine could hear,
(And not without a passing thrill of fear),
The sliding bolt, the key that she withdrew:
He might be safe, but was a captive, too.

When food and wine had done their kindly best
For his spent strength, Romaine sank down to rest.
Long and refreshing was his deep repose:
Then, sleep to slumber changed; wild dreams arose;
Strange forms of death and terror: all in vain
He strove to break the dream so full of pain;
The vision came again, and yet again;—
A woman's threatening beauty, bright and fierce
As polished poniards, glittering while they pierce;
A face with gleaming eye and cruel lip,
That mocked him till he started from his sleep.

XVI.

Down from the center of the ceiling hung
A lamp beneath a milk-white shade, that flung
A mild and moonlight radiance o'er the room,
Nor left a nook nor corner in the gloom.
Romaine could see no window anywhere;
The room, indeed, was, like the secret stair,
Built in the thickness of the old brick walls,
And filched from closets in the long, dark halls.
Yet, though there was no window, fresh and free

The air passed in and out: he could not see
Whence came the wind, but felt upon his brow
Its cooling breath; beheld it fluttering now
In the dark folds of something on the wall—
Something that waved with gentle rise and fall,
Like a thin curtain swaying to the wind:
Perhaps, a window might be hid behind!
Upspringing from his couch, Romaine advanced
And drew the curtain—stood, as one entranced!

XVII.

He did not find a curtained window there,
But a bright, pictured form, supremely fair;
The full-length portrait of a lovely girl.
Her left hand, lightly drooping, held the whorl
Of a great lily; her right hand, thrown high
Above her head, held there exultingly
A cluster of wild grapes, whose trailing vine
Curled its light tendrils round her fingers fine,
Shadowed the outline of her snowy arm,
And circled half the figure's airy charm.
So light the pose, so small the fairy foot,
So glad the face beneath the o'erhanging fruit,
She seemed the spirit of some flowering wood,
Where wild grapes hang in purple plenitude.
Rose-white were rounded arms, and neck, and brow,
As morning's blush upon new-fallen snow;
Rose-red the smiling lips; and dimples break
The rose-bloom shadows of the lovely cheek.

The soft, rich blackness of the starry eyes
Shone through dark lashes, on whose chestnut dyes
Lay tints of dusky gold, as if they strove
To harmonize with slender brows above,
Drawn in straight lines of palest golden-brown,
Yet darker than the hair, her beauty's crown.
Light-gold the tresses whose redundant flow
Swept over snowy shoulders, far below
The slender girdle, shimmering, floating far:
As in the rising mist the morning-star
Shines nebulous and golden through the veil
Whose hazy web enfolds her splendors pale,
So shone the form, whose flossy, floating hair
Hung like a golden gauze upon the air.

Although the further slumbers of Romaine
Were filled with dreams, they were not dreams of pain;
Nor did Marcella haunt him: in her place
He saw the pictured beauty's radiant face.

XVIII.

When he awoke, it might have been broad day
Without, but of the sunlight not a ray
Entered that close apartment. Still the light
Swung, that illumed the chamber through the night,
But last night's feast had been removed; and there
A negro stood, beside the easy chair,
Who, when he saw the youth unclose his eyes,
Moved forward: "When it pleases you to rise,

I'm here to serve you, sir; King is my name,
And you may trust me, sir, the very same,
Like as Marcella or Miss Adelaide.
Your breakfast waits for you; the coffee's made."

After repast, the picture smiling there
Drew Romaine's gaze; the picture with bright hair.
"King, tell me, if you can—what picture's this?"
"That, sir, is our Miss Blanche, our own young Miss,
Old Mistis' niece, and long her favorite.
Park Aubray ought to be hers now, by right;
Not but Miss Blanche had money of her own—
Beg pardon, sir! It's time I should be gone,
If you have nothing more for me to do.
My mistis' soon will come to visit you."
"Where is *she*, now?"
      Miss Blanche? Nobody knows.
Some neither know nor care, as I suppose!
Money makes folks hard-hearted, seems to me.
They say, Miss Blanche has gone to Italy,
A foreign country, sir. They say, her home
Is in some town—I think they call it, Rome.—
But, hark! I hear Miss Ad'laide."
        At the name,
A knock was heard: into the room then came
Adelaide and Marcella. King withdrew.

Long talked the cousins; each for each went through
The history of the past three years; and then

Spoke of the present. What was best, or when
Romaine should leave Park Aubray, was not clear.
He was both tired and ill, and *must* rest here
Until his strength returned, and he could try
Once more to pass the hostile boundary.

Adelaide had not, hitherto, beheld
The portrait, though its beauty hung unveiled;
But when the conversation flagged, Romaine
Said: "Beauty has no charms for you, 'tis plain!
How long could you remain here, cousin mine,
Without one glance to give that face divine?"

Adelaide started, turned and looked askance
Upon the portrait, with a darkling glance,
As if on something hateful to her view.

"The sweetest face that ever painter drew!"
Romaine continued. "Cousin, on my word,
I credit not a whisper I have heard
Against Blanche Aubray. Such a girl must be
As bright as light, true as fidelity!"

"Blanche Aubray is a *woman*, now; 'tis long
Since that was painted."
     "She has had great wrong!
What if she were an abolitionist?
Should she, for such a cause, be so dismissed
From home and friends? The better, if 'tis true!
Love, honor, reverence, are still more her due,

At least, from Northern—"
              "Cease!" the lady cried:
" *That* was not all! There's worse, *much* worse, beside!
Have you not heard—"
                    "Yes, Adelaide! I know
That when Blanche Aubray fled from shame and woe
'Twas said, she took with her both gems and gold
Committed to her care, and laces old,
And priceless manuscripts of unknown age,
And other trumpery. I burn with rage
And blush with shame, to think of calumny
So vile! I scorn the story utterly!
When war is past, and order comes again,"
Thus eagerly resumed the young Romaine,
With sparkling eyes and warmly flushing cheek;
"'This beautiful, this injured girl I'll seek—
Yes, I will seek her through the living world!"
Adelaide spoke not, but her lip was curled,
And she, with eyes averted, scornful air,
Turned from the dark-eyed portrait with gold hair.
But, on the lady's arm her cousin laid
His hand, and pointing to the picture, said:
"You, cousin— *you* will surely join with me
To right her wrongs—"
                    "If any wrongs there be!"
Coldly said Adelaide. "You dream, Romaine!
These are the fancies of a fevered brain:
You should not talk, but rest, I well perceive.

I'll see you, soon, again."
      She took her leave,
And, followed by Marcella, left the place.
Romaine still gazed upon the pictured face.

CANTO III.

I.

Two weeks went by, while, racked with fever-pain
And sick almost to dying, lay Romaine:
The crisis past; and to his wasted frame
His health and strength once more, but slowly, came.

Now, Adelaide's birthday came; a day when she
Each year received a chosen company;
And so, though ill at ease, and sad at heart,
She now prepared to play the hostess' part,
Lest prying friends and neighbors wonder why
She did not entertain as formerly.
The feast was made; the flower-wreathed rooms below
Were filling fast; gay words and laughter flow:
But a "poor cousin," whom she patronized,
Received the lady's guests; apologized,
With many smiles, for Adelaide's delay:
And the good natured crowd was pleased to say
Adelaide, of this birthday-feast the queen,
Should choose her time to join the festal scene.

II.

Before her mirror still sate Adelaide.
Her shining hair in one great crowning-braid
Marcella gathered: two escaping curls
Dropped on her neck; and strings of glistening pearls
Held in their wreathing lustre every fold
Of the dark-gleaming locks of chestnut-gold:
Pearls ringed her snowy throat, her slender zone,
And at each ear in trembling beauty shone.
Her satin robe, (than frozen snow more white,)
Fell in rich, glittering folds and curves of light;
And on her breast a cluster-diamond glows,—
One touch of fire in all those pearls and snows.

III.

Why does the lady linger? Why should she
Neglect so long the expectant company.
Waiting her coming in the rooms below?
Why burns upon her cheek the fever-glow
That gives her faultless lip its scarlet dye,
And lends new lustre to her violet eye?

The lady sees, within the mirror wide,
Her own bright figure and her maid's beside.
The silver-tasseled jacket of rich blue,
The silken turban of the same bright hue,
Became Marcella's form of airy grace,
And heightened the dark beauty of her face;
And bright with strange emotion was the glance

Fixed on her lady's mirrored countenance.
Reflected in the mirror, Adelaide
Beheld the brilliant beauty of her maid,
A loveliness that into shadow threw
Her fairer features and less vivid hue.
The lady looked upon her earnestly:
The maid returned the gaze with steadfast eye.

IV.

"Marcella!" in suppressed and trembling tone
Her mistress spoke. "Marcella! it is known—
Known to my husband that Romaine is here!
My brain is almost wild with rage and fear!
Romaine, my cousin, must take instant flight—
My husband will be here to-morrow-night!"

"Can this be true? How have you been betrayed?"
"I know not—but 'tis true!" said Adelaide.
"I have it from a friend I cannot doubt.
Some prying wretch has traced the secret out,
Or, King himself, perhaps—"
"That cannot be!"
Replied Marcella. "King would fain be free,
And would, I think, be always blindly true
To anything that wore the Yankee blue.—
The major comes, you say, to-morrow-night?"

"Yes! Think for me—I am bewildered quite,
And maddened with suspense! *Your* head is clear,
And cool, and calm: you have no sense of fear!

You know my cousin's peril—and for me,
Think of my husband's frantic jealousy,
Like a wild fever raging in his blood:—
Help; if you owe me love or gratitude!"

" Go down to meet the assembled company,"
Replied Marcella, " and leave all to me.
You may believe me fully, when I say,
All that I owe to you I will repay!"

V.

Not one among her guests was half so gay
As Adelaide, queen of the festal day;
No smiling eye gave out so bright a glance;
No foot more lightly twinkled through the dance;
And none more fully, freely joined than she
In the light war of wit and raillery.
Marcella's keen, cold eye took in the scene
As near the door she stood; composed, serene,
As if love, hatred, jealous anger, were
Nothing to any, least of all to her.
She stood not with the servants in the hall;
(Indeed, she mingled not with them at all,
At any time; and they, with hate and fear,
Shrank from her glittering glance and brow severe).
Often, within the parlors Adelaide
Required attendance of her favorite maid;
And there, apart, she held her usual place,
With well-assured but unobtrusive grace.

VI.

The dances ended, wit and laughter flowed:
Then music for a season held the crowd.
" A song!" they all petitioned Adelaide.
" A sad or merry song?" the lady said.
Laughingly, they responded, " Glad and gay!
We would forget all sorrow, for one day!"
Lightly her hands across the harp-strings glide,
And the sweet notes flowed like a rippling tide.

1.

"Merry and glad are the days we've had,
    And the beautiful months in going
All glide along like sounds of song
    From the lips of music flowing;
The song of Time is a tuneful rhyme,
And days, like bells with a silver chime,
Ring in the prime of flower-wreathed Time,
    When the rose of life is glowing.

2.

Then smile to-day, while yet you may,
    Nor from the future borrow
One shade of fear: when joy is here,
    We will not dream of sorrow!
Beauty is here, and Love is near;
The stream of time runs nectar-clear,
For Hope is here, and Mirth and Cheer,
    To sing of a brighter morrow!"

This song was at the closing of the feast.
Adelaide smiled on the last parting guest,
And turning, met Marcella's gleaming eye,
To which excitement gave wild brilliancy.
"Lady! I have a word for your own ear:
The message said, *to-morrow* will bring here
Your husband; but the word was not aright:
Madame, your husband will be here this night!
You may rely on me that *this* is true.
We must do quickly what we have to do!
Go to your room; and do not yet despair!
In a few moments I will join you there."

VII.

Within her room not long the lady sate,
In wild suspense her slave's approach to wait;
Although, in moments of such agony,
An hour is foretaste of eternity.
At last, Marcella came—ah, no, not she!
Rather, some fiend of subtle mockery.
Still on her head the gaudy turban shines,
And dark above the straight, black eye-brow-lines
The silken fringe of jetty ringlets lies,
Shading the cruel splendors of her eyes;
But from her cheek the dusky bloom has flown,
And whither has the brown complexion gone?
Throughout the world, the eye might vainly seek
A whiter rose than lies on that smooth cheek;

Her throat, her slender hands, are pure as snow,
And lilies are no fairer than her brow.

Upsprang with beating heart, pale Adelaide!
Trembling, aghast, she looked upon the maid.
"Do you not know me yet?" Marcella said:
"Do not my voice, complexion, *all*—proclaim,
Before I utter it, my hated name?

VIII.

"Of all the wretches born, I do believe
Deceivers are the easiest to deceive!
You thought I was Marcella, in good sooth?
Never so much as dimly guessed the truth?
Your grateful slave, the fond, the true, the tried,
For three long years was ever at your side;
In all that time did no responsive chord
Thrill to my touch? Did no half-uttered word,
No trick of voice, of movement shape, or eye,
Arouse your doubt or wake your memory?
Could you believe, a slave who once had earned
Her freedom, ever truly could have yearned
For bondage, or would freely take the chain
And willingly lift up the cross again?
Natural! to give up life's best hopes; to brave
The lash, the living death, to be—*your slave!*

"Yet, I remember in your blooming youth,
You *had* one friend who worshiped you in truth!

A friend, who, blinded by your matchless art
Gave you her fullest trust, her inmost heart:
Faith, trust, and boundless love to you she gave,
And would have been—she *was*—your willing slave!
The Present shall take hands with that dead Past—
Behold your much-loved, long-lost friend, at last!"

IX.

She raised the silken turban from her head,
And with it came the fringe of curls: instead
Of crispy, jet-black ringlets, fold on fold
Lay massive coils of hair of palest gold,
Above a noble forehead, broad and high,
And smoothly white as polished ivory.
She loosened the rich hair, that falling spread
In silky fleece, a mass of golden thread;
In lovely length and peerless quantity,
It hung, a glittering veil, from brow to knee.

"Of fortune, friends, and reputation shorn,
You sent me from the house where I was born!
Not for lost wealth I grieve: to prove you true,
I would have yielded home and fortune, too,
Though the least flower that grows on Aubray land
Is more to me than you can understand.
You stole the heart whose love had been to me
Even as a mother's, from my infancy;
Poisoned her doting mind with the belief
That I was what *you* were—and *are*—a thief!

You turned her love to hate; and, more than all,
You turned my own heart's blood to bitterest gall!

X.

"Some women to a lover give the heart
In their fond youth; some choose the better part,
And yield to heaven the adoration due;
But *all* adore some god, or false, or true;
All have an idol at whose shrine they bend—
I worshiped not a lover, but a *friend!*

"'Pity' and 'pardon' you? Why, so I do!
I stand, now, on the same low plane with you,
And so we two on equal terms can meet.
I meant that you should lie thus at my feet,
Like the crushed worm you are; and I meant, too,
To strike you through the life most dear to you;
To see *you* drink of that envenomed bowl
Which *I* have drained in bitterness of soul!
But, shall your wretched influence destroy
Two bright young lives? No! I will save this boy!
Many, as hard, as shallow-brained as you,
In their own way, would brand me as untrue
To my own land, and traitorous to the South,
In snatching thus from death a Northern youth;
And there are others, on the Union side,
Who for this deed would hold me glorified.
But country, patriotism, State, and all
Such sounding echoes from the dead Past fall
Idly upon my ear: I stand alone :

Home, brotherhood, or country, I have none!
And, if I save Romaine, 'tis not, in truth,
Because I love, or hate, the North, or South:
I, homeless, nameless, loveless—what to me
Is any Union or Confederacy?

"Heed what I say! To-night, your angry lord
Will search the house. I pledge an Aubray's word,
That he shall find *me* in that secret room,
And not your Northern cousin. I presume,
Unless your talents for intrigue are lost,
You'll frame some specious tale: count not the cost
To *me*—but *that*, I know, you will not do:
Say what you will, and I'll avouch it true.
Tell him, Blanche Aubray is the hidden spy—
Or say what pleases you: I'll naught deny.

XI.

"I'm strangely cold and weary, and I long
Only for rest: remembrance of my wrong
Fades, in this strange indifference of my mind,
And hate is dead as love and hope. I find
Revenge not sweet but tasteless. You, no doubt,
Had you begun this game, would play it out!
You won a deeper game, in days gone by—
Played for high stakes, and won by treachery.
I am ashamed, not that I loved, at first,
But, that through long and weary years I've nursed
So great a hatred for so small a thing!

Thin streams must flow from such a feeble spring;
Yet, from this brackish well I sought, (poor fool!)
Sweet waters, healing as Siloam's pool!
You won the stake you played for in your youth,
And yet, I do not envy you, in truth!
Three years, your daily life I've closely scanned;
Your panting heart lies naked in my hand;
And a base heart it is, whose every beat
Is thick with servile fear or planned deceit.
Too meanly selfish, far too cold and faint,
For a great sinner or a gracious saint,
Conscience and soul you have, but each so small,
It were far better you had none, at all:
Too weak to be restraints they keep your will
Swaying uneasily from good to ill,
And false to everything. I would not be
The thing you are, for heaven's eternity!"

XII.

She ceased. There came, down the long avenue,
The sound of trampling hoofs, that nearer drew;
Then shouts, and baying dogs, and mingling noise.

"'They come—*he* comes! I hear my husband's voice!"
Cried frantic Adelaide; and, kneeling, flung
Her arms around Blanche Aubray's knees, and clung
With upturned features whiter than the dead.

" Blanche! Dearest Blanche! Save *him!* But now, you said
You'd save Romaine, but how—"

"'The cellar-stair
Is guarded, but there is a pass elsewhere.
I know this house—ah! none so well as I!
My life for his, your kinsman shall not die!
Time presses—smooth that face to meet your lord,
And, for the rest, you have Blanche Aubray's word!"

She said: and passing quickly from the room,
Vanished, amid the long hall's dusky gloom.

XIII.

This scene, of such importance to Romaine,
Passed while the midnight hour was on the wane,
When, in the secret room's security,
And all unconscious of the danger nigh,
He rested, safe but lonely. All day long,
And half the night, came softened sounds of song,
Music, and laughter, from the rooms below:
He heard the sound of wheels that come and go,
And voices of the merry groups that rove
Through the gay garden and the lighted grove;
He felt the floor vibrate to dancing feet,
When harp and violin, in concert sweet,
Made music thrilling to the youthful heart:
And then, he heard the merry guests depart,

With laughter, jest, and mingling voices gay,
And rolling wheels, that echoed far away.

This later, slighter noise, of trampling steed
And barking dogs, he did not hear, or heed.
Looking upon the picture's radiant face,
Romaine stood dreaming of poor Blanche. His gaze
Was fixed so long, the wavering sight grew dim,
And the bright form seemed gliding off from him,—
Wavered, and moved, and paused. It could not be—
But, yes, it moved, it trembled visibly.
Half startled, he beheld the portrait glide
Steadily to the left: an opening wide
Led to the outer air, for he could feel
Cool winds of midnight through the apartment steal.
But, in this open window suddenly
A phantom seemed to stand: such it must be;
Or had the enchanted portrait left its place?
There was the white-rose beauty of the face,
The bright redundance of the matchless hair—
But not the portrait's eyes that glittered there!

XIV.

Startled beyond his self-control, the youth
Half-thought he saw a spirit-form, in truth;
And, part in awe, and part in ecstasy,
With hands extended, sank upon his knee.

"Rise! rise, I pray you, sir! You have no time
For raptures or heroic pantomime.
Speak not, but listen! You must flee, this night,
From Aubray. To direct and aid your flight,
The faithful King your journey shall attend.
If you in Northern lands should prove his friend,
I will account it service done to me.—
(I am Blanche Aubray, whom your chivalry
So lately burned to serve). Beyond the mere
Fleet horses wait your coming. Stay not here!
Never was there more danger in delay—
Death tracks you as a sleuth-hound tracks his prey!"

"Strange being! And as beautiful as strange!
I am not blinded by this wondrous change;
Those are Marcella's eyes, though softened so,—
And, more than all, Marcella's voice I know,
For never voice had such a golden ring
Since birds of Paradise have ceased to sing!
Blanche Aubray? Where, then, is the soul that lies
In the soft radiance of the pictured eyes?
Why this deception? Why this mean disguise?"

"Disguise is at an end with me; but you
Must wear one yet, to help you safely through
A journey of such peril. Come! Once more
Trust to my guidance, as you did before.
Trust me! With confidence this claim I make,

Not for my own but for Blanche Aubray's sake,
The artist's vision, there, in oil and paint,
That your young fancy worshiped as a saint."

"But you, Marcella—do you not incur
Danger, if I should fly? I should prefer
Death at the hangman's hands, if I but thought—"

"There is no danger, save to you! Speak not,
But go! For every moment that you stay,
You throw ten chances for your life away!"

XV.

She caught his arm, and drew him hurriedly
Through the wide window to a balcony
All shadowed in the wreathing trumpet-vines,
Through whose thick sprays the full moon faintly shines.
Then the thick vines were parted, and a voice
Breathed low: "Miss Blanche!"

"Make not the slightest noise!"
She answered King, as low. "Here's gold for you—
Be faithful, free, and prosperous. Adieu!"

Through the half-parted vines, Romaine can see
A ladder placed against the balcony.
To this she motioned him. He looked again,
With a strange thrill of tenderness and pain,
Upon the sad, bright being at his side,

And tried to speak, and twice in vain he tried.
At last, he took her hand in both his own:
"Marcella!" he began with faltering tone;
"Blanche Aubray! your past life I cannot trace,
But suffering has made grand that lovely face:
Ah, deep, indeed, your sorrow must have been,
Not through your own, but through another's sin!
I partly guess the truth—yet, I implore,
That for past wrong you seek revenge no more!
You shall have justice, be it soon or late.—
Tell me, should *I* add to your sorrow's weight,
Or bring on you some danger by my flight?
If so, I should far rather die this night!"

" By your *delay* my sufferings are increased;
O let me save *your* bright young life, at least!
I see you young and hopeful; think you true;
Modest, I know, and gentle-hearted, too.—
No longer here the flying moments waste,
But leave this place at once, and that with haste!"

He kissed with reverent lips the hand that lay
Cold in his own; and, turning, went his way.
Breathless, she watched and waited, till she knew
They were beyond the mere. Deep breath she drew
When the wild signal-cry, the whippowil,
Three times resounded from the Cedar Hill:
Then she regained, once more, the secret room,
And waited there, in darkness and in gloom.

XVI.

Meanwhile, with heart and spirit all aflame
With jealous anger, Major Lovelace came
To his wife's chamber.   Adelaide arose:
Her features she had masked in forced repose,
Had stilled her trembling lips, and to her eyes
Called up a look of pleasure and surprise.
But he, with flushing brow and "eye of death,"
Cried: "Stay! No nearer come! and spare your breath
The uttering of falsehoods: all too late
They come, to save your lover from his fate!"

"My lover!   Do you speak these words to *me?*—
And wherefore come you home so suddenly,
And in such anger?"

            "Adelaide, be wise!
Useless is falsehood, vain is artifice.
I know that you have hidden in this house,
For two weeks space, at least, my loyal spouse!
A Yankee spy—"

            "Not so! my cousin, sir!
I do confess, my cousin now is here,
As you perhaps have heard;—"
            "Then you deny
That you have hidden here a Northern spy?"

" Indeed, I do deny it!"
"We shall see!
That hidden room shall open presently—"

"The sooner, Charles, the better, too, for me!
But, heed well what you do—perhaps you may
Regret both word and deed, another day!
Soon, you will know *who* is the 'hidden spy'
Whose presence here has raised your wrath so high."

"Give me the hall-key! for I fain would see,"
He said, "Your hidden treasure.—Follow me!"
At these last words, he opened wide the door;
And through the soft, luxurious chamber pour
Unwonted guests: two rough, strong men in grey,
Confederate soldiers, forward lead the way;
A group of servants following silently,
Scared, but agape with curiosity.

XVII.

The hall had, at one end, a winding stair
Above a long, wide closet. Pausing there—
"A soldier guards," said Lovelace, "that small door
That leads into the cellar; on this floor
There is no entrance to this secret den
Save through this closet. Stand here, you two men,
And, on your lives, let not a soul pass through
Till I command. But all the rest of you

Into this closet follow me."
                    They did,
Eager to see the apartment so long hid,
Park Aubray's "ghost-room." Superstition said,
Each night the spirits of the Aubray dead
There held high revel; for, as midnight came,
Each Aubray portrait, stepping from its frame,
To the long-hidden ghost-room hied away,
And reveled there until the dawning day.

Lovelace walked first, and Adelaide came last:
With head erect and haughty step she passed.
Bright were the deep-blue eyes, for shining there
Was the dark, dangerous courage of despair;
And all the clustered diamonds on her breast
Trembled and sparkled to its wild unrest.

XVIII.

They reached the portal of the hidden room,
And, with a blow fierce as the stroke of doom,
Lovelace burst in the door. Then forward sprung
A figure to resist him—lightly flung
A veil before his eyes—and from his hand
Struck down the light. All in thick darkness stand,
Confused and frightened, though they see not who
Or what put out the light; but Lovelace drew
His pistol, as enraged he shouted: "Yield!
Coward, the darkness shall not be your shield!"

The light was stricken from his hand, but not
Before the eye a golden gleam had caught,
Shining against rich blue, which, sure, must be
The gold-laced garment of his enemy;
And, maddening at the thought, he did not stay
For light, but rushed straight forward: in his way
He almost fell against a form that tried
To shun his grasp, but vainly. "Yield!" he cried;
"Speak! or I shoot you where you stand!"
        A shriek
From Adelaide rang through the apartment.
       "Speak!"
Again cried Lovelace. Leaving in his clasp
A silken sash, the figure fled his grasp.
Then rang a pistol-shot—a flash—a fall—
Then one faint groan—a sob—and that was all.
Silence and darkness.
     "Haste to bring a light!"
Said Lovelace All was wonder and affright,
And, some wild moments, dire confusion reigned;
But, each, with torch or candle armed, regained
His courage, and pressed forward to that room,
Forever after cursed with triple gloom.

XIX.

For, veiled in rich profusion of bright hair,
It was a woman who lay dying there,
A woman whom, at once, all recognize.

Silent, they gasp with horror and surprise,
As crowding torches pour a fiery flood
Upon Blanche Aubray and the welling blood
That flowed amain with every shortening breath:
The soldiers paled, though used to look on death.
Beneath her own young portrait, fallen she lay;
And to that pictured form the flickering play
Of light and shadow seeming motion lent,
As if her guardian seraph o'er her bent;
In such unchanging loveliness it stands,
Like a bright visitant from heavenly lands,
Waiting to share immortal youth and peace
With the twin-soul that death must soon release.

Aghast at his own work, her slayer stood
Spell-bound, and gazed upon the welling blood;
Then, as a cry of horror and amaze
Broke from his pallid lips, he strove to raise
The dying girl,—but "No;" she gently said;
"I am already numbered with the dead,
So let me part in peace."
     He knelt, and took
Her icy hand in one as cold, which shook,
As hers did not.
     "If you," she said, "would have
Forgiveness for this deed, one boon I crave,
My last request."
     "Oh Blanche, you *must not die!*

Ask what you will—but yield not thus! Oh, *try*,
For *my* sake, try to call back life again,—
Oh heaven! to bear the heavy curse of Cain!"

She turned on him her deep and solemn eye:
"As you hope mercy, seek not to know *why*
You find me at Park Aubray; nor upbraid
With this night's work my cousin Adelaide."

He could not answer her in words, but pressed
Her small, cold hand against his troubled breast.

XX.

But, now, with reeling step, wild Adelaide
Came forward. "Let me speak with her!" she said.
"For heaven's love, let me speak with her alone!"
They all drew back, even Lovelace; so that none
Might hear. With trembling hand she strove to staunch
The fatal wound with the long hair of Blanche
"I have not *murdered* you? Oh try to live!
Blanche, you once loved—have *saved* me—Oh, *forgive!*

A momentary gleam of faint surprise
Came o'er Blanche Aubray's face: she raised her eyes:
Her whole heart-history was in that gaze—
The boundless love, the trust of other days;
Then, a wild look of bitter agony
Shone in strange splendor from the speaking eye,
An agony whose fullness none might guess:
And then, a look of utter weariness.

Upon the calm, pale features slowly grows
That still, sad fixedness of deep repose;
On the dark eyes the weary eyelids fall,
And Death's pale shadow settles over all.

The sunrise through the open window came,
Filling the room with its pale-rosy flame.
It tinged the portrait rosy-red, and flushed
The dead girl's cheek, as if she faintly blushed;
Brightened the calm, broad brow, so deadly-fair,
And glittered on the shroud of golden hair—
That wondrous growth of flossy gold, that shone
Even now, with life and lustre all its own;
But the strong soul that loved and suffered so
Had fled to its eternal weal or woe.

END OF MARCELLA.

NOTES TO MARCELLA.

CANTO I.

1. IV. "*A grove of Spanish oaks, whose branches threw.*"

The tree called Spanish-oak in Piedmont-Virginia, seems rather to be the *Quercus coccinea* of botanists; a beautiful oak, noted for its rich, glossy-green leaves, which turn bright crimson in autumn.

2. VII. "*And low-born culture eyed with calm disdain.*"

It is well known that an overweening pride of birth was the most prominent weakness of the blue-blood families of Virginia; a pride that scorned mere wealth; and, while regarding talent or culture with more respect than riches, yet, there were certain defects of birth for which not the greatest genius or highest culture could compensate. *All* the true aristocrats of the Old Dominion, however, did not carry this family pride to such length.

3. XI. "*An abolitionist.*"

To those who understand anything of the feeling of the Old South toward an abolitionist—synonym for incendiary, conspirator, spy, and even infidel, in the Southern vocabulary—it will not seem surprising that a person supposed to be in league with abolitionists, or to hold abolition doctrines—as Southrons believed them—it cannot be surprising, we repeat, or at all unnatural that the suspected person should be disgraced and ostracized both by personal friends and the general public. *Two* such cases, one of great cruelty, are known by the author to have occurred just before the late Civil War. The continual and most terrible fear of an insurrection is one of the innumerable woes and curses attending on slavery—a fear affecting equally the guilty and the innocent, pro-slavey slave-holders, and, not less, anti-slavery inheritors of slaves.

CANTO II.

1. III. "*Trembled across the mere.*"

Mere is a name very commonly given, in the Piedmont section of Virginia, to a *winding* body of water, too still and sluggish for a creek, too narrow and meandering for a pond. As most of the streams in that hilly region are *torrents*, and most pools either valley-lakes or mountain-tarns, a mere is not commonly seen, unless artificially produced, for picturesque effect, on ornamented plantations of the extinct class of aristocratic planters.

2. III. "*Wild ivy.*"

Piedmont name for kalmia laurel.

3. IV. "*Sweet-brake*

A species of wood-fern, beautiful, and very fragrant; often called *sweet-fern*, but not the sweet-fern proper.

4. X. "*Not like a common slave was she arrayed.*

Marcella's costume, which might well be considered too rich and *Oriental* for Virginia, was copied from the attire of a young quadroon, worn during the war; except that *blue* has been substituted for crimson, in the colors. It was the time of zouave jackets, semi-military gilt buttons, tinsel braid, etc.; and no slave's costume was complete without as rich a turban as she could procure. The graceful and picturesque turban, however, has disappeared with slavery.

CANTO III.

1. VIII. *" You thought I was Marcella, in good sooth?"*

Such a deception as here shown was easy enough to be practiced on the owner of several plantations—or even *one* large one—containing hundreds of slaves, neither knowing the master nor known by him. Indeed, slaves on these inherited, over-stocked plantations, (crowded with negroes of all ages,) usually knew their master *by sight* much more frequently than the master could possibly know the slave. The supposed deception could be carried on with scarcely a possibility of suspicion, if, as in the case of *Marcella*, the fugitive had fled while yet not grown, remained away years, and returned—as imagined—not to the plantation where she had been known as a child, but to a mistress who had never seen her, among servants who, if they had ever seen, had certainly no familiar knowledge of her person or disposition. In personating *Marcella*, Blanche had but to thoroughly disguise *herself*.

WILD IRIS:

AND

OTHER RHYMES OF CHILDHOOD AND YOUTH.

WILD IRIS AND OTHER RHYMES.

WILD IRIS.

(1862.)

The iris in the Southland opens early:
    When the first hint of green the willows take,
The leafless alders hang their tassels merely,
    Till spice and maple in the March winds shake,
    And the azalea reddens all the brake;
Then the magnolia-buds grow round and pearly,
    And the wild iris blossoms by the lake.

O beautiful blue iris! best and dearest,
    Save the wild ivy,* of all vernal bloom!
Not winter's chill nor wild spring-rain thou fearest,
    Nor rush of swollen torrents, white with foam;
    For, by the brooklet is thy chosen home,
And all the lowlands flush when thou appearest,
    With heart of gold beneath an azure plume.

Who, that has seen the Southern meadows glowing
    With iris, brighter than the bluebird's wing,

---

* "Wild ivy," *i, e.*, the kalmia laurel, called "wild ivy" throughout Virginia and North Carolina, where, also, one species of azalea is known only as "wild honey-suckle." The common wild coral-honeysuckle, a *true* honeysuckle, they have named "woodbine."

But felt his heart with rapture overflowing,
   And blessed the Maker of so fair a thing!
   For, who loves beauty must love beauty's King—
Almighty Monarch, in his grace bestowing
   Such wealth of beauty on a flower of spring.

THE RIVER.

(June, 1858.)

We stood upon the hill's green slope;
   A moonlit sky was smiling o'er us,
And, like the illusive rays of hope,
   The gleaming fire-flies danced before us:
There gently flowed thy rippling tide,
   In liquid light, with restless quiver;
Green willows grace thy winding side,
              Bright-flowing river.

And all was silence, deep, profound,
   Save one wild horn, by distance mellow,
And thine own soft and murmuring sound,
   Rippling around the isles of willow,
Or wild, sweet strain that o'er thee floats,
   To die away, returning never;
Mingling with thy soft-swelling notes,
              Murmuring river!

O! were the stream of time like thee,

Whose every wavelet sings with gladness,
  Could sorrow, as the moonbeams, flee,
    Nor leave behind one trace of sadness—
How sweetly could our frail barque rest
  Upon such crested waves forever,
Or float on such a shining breast,
              Beautiful river!

TO MY BROTHER.

(Oct. 15, 1859.)

Do you remember, when the twilight, stealing
  Softly around our childhood's forest home;
And the young crescent-moon, her form revealing,
  Tipped with a tender light the yellow broom—
When the tall pines, their fragrant odors blending,
  Sighed gently to the rocking of the wind,
How far our gipsy feet, the foot-path wending,
  Left dwelling-house and cabins all behind?
      Do you remember?

Can you forget how, hand in hand, we wandered
  Through fields of waving wheat and tasseled corn,
And gathered fox-grapes where the brook meandered,
  Called homeward only by the dinner-horn?
Then, the old mill—how well we loved its clatter,
  And its great wheel with steps so like a stair!

How would I strive, in childish mirth, to scatter
   The sparkling water on your soft, brown hair!
     Do you remember?

And the fine group of ruddy maples, drooping
   Their rosy clusters o'er our dear old spring;
The graceful fringe-tree's snowy tassels, stooping
   Their trembling shadows on the brook to fling;
And the steep hill-side, with the green moss spreading
   Its velvet cushion in our favorite nook!
While I reclined upon its bosom, reading,
   You fished for minnows in the quiet brook.
     Do you remember?

And when the summer's garlands all had faded,
   When autumn's gaudy blossoms ceased to bloom;
When leafless boughs no more our footsteps shaded,
   And odorous pines made sweet the forest gloom;
How did we wander then, so wild and merry,
   Through rustling leaves, and naked, pathless wood,
Seeking the holly for its scarlet berry,
   And Solomon's seal, with berries red as blood.
     Do you remember?

And when the winter nights came, chill and snowing,
   We gathered round the blazing wood-fire warm,
And heard the whistling winds so roughly blowing,
   And the wild howling of the outside storm—
We played our simple, childish games, and nightly

Related wondrous goblin-tales of fear;
Carved pigmy boats, and built cob-houses tightly,
  With lightwood torches for our chandelier!
      Do you remember?

Three years have passed since then, and I am sighing
  For the bright days that can return no more :
Bright childhood will not stay, for all our crying—
  But flowery paths of youth are on before!
Brother, your young heart still retains its childhood;
  And all the pleasant ways we used to roam,
In the green fields and through the bloomy wildwood
  That circled round our early forest-home,
      You will remember.

AMID THE CORN.

(Dec. 28th, 1859.)

Amid the rows of rustling corn,
    Whose saber-leaves so lightly swung,
And from whose tops, that dewy morn,
          Silk tassels hung,

They sat; and the old chestnut-tree
    Over the corn-tops cast a shade :
Those long, white blooms how gracefully
          The light wind swayed!

They wove a wreath of flowers that grew
    Within that grassy, shaded place,
But fairer still, to Hubert's view,
        Was Linda's face.

Eyes like the morning-glories blue;
    Bright as the corn-silk was her hair:
The slipping lizard stopped to view
        A face so fair!

They planned their future golden hours,
    With glowing hopes, that sunny morn.
And braided thick the wreath of flowers,
        Down in the corn.

Nine years have passed: he stands alone
    Where last he sat by Linda's side.
How many hopes have come and gone,
        Have bloomed and died!

The autumn-leaves are crisp and sear,
    The yellow grasses softly wave
On fields that spread, all bare and drear,
        Round Linda's grave:

The chestnut leaves fall slowly down;
    Over the withered blooms they spread,
And weave a pall of gold-and-brown
        Above the dead.

Sweet Linda's was a bitter fate,
 And death in kindness to her came;
And Hubert knows the price (too late)
   Of earthly fame.

The chain they linked with future hours
 And golden hopes, that happy morn,
Has faded with the wreath of flowers,
   Down in the corn.

ELLEN.

(Oct., 1860.)

The poplar waves his golden crown
 Through all the Indian-summer day;
The ruby oak-leaves shower down
 Upon the grave of Ellen Ray.

A purple mist is in the air;
 The woods are bright with autumn's dyes;
The windy mountain-tops are bare;
 And from the tree the rain-frog cries.

Her grave is at the garden's foot:
 The weed-grown flowers have run to waste;
And wandering vines with leaf and shoot
 Have crossed the gate and bound it fast.

Forsaken the lone house remains;
 The swallows cluster round the eaves,

And o'er the shattered window-panes
  Her silver web the spider weaves.

From the old roof, moss-grown and thin,
  Projects a window, open wide;
And dusky bats flit out and in
  The lonely room where Ellen died.

Thick bind-weeds choke the path she made
  To the wood-fountain clear and cool;
The timid hare is not afraid
  To drink beside the dimpling pool.

The black-snake's glittering folds may twine
  Beneath the jasmine drooping there,
Whose milk-white blooms were wont to shine
  In Ellen's braids of dark-brown hair.

The roses that she loved to train
  Have died by her deserted door:
They will revive with summer's rain,
  But Ellen Ray will wake no more.

THE LILY QUEEN.

(1861.)

She stood in the flowering forest,
  Alone by the side of the lakelet,
    Alone in the wild, haunted wood.
She had come when her sorrow was sorest,

For one effort more she would make yet.
    To hold the false love, to make good
The bond that no power could break yet.

The forest lay hushed in deep silence:
    The magical charm had been muttered;
        The wood-creatures fled in alarm;
The lake-lilies, fairy-like islands,
    Lay lifeless; no forest-bird uttered
        A warble to break the wild charm;
No leaf on the lily-trees fluttered.

The lily-queen rises in brightness,
    Where the magnolia is throwing
        Shadows on water and land:
She is white with an ivory whiteness,
    And fair are the tresses free-flowing;
        She holds a green rod in her hand,
That is topped by a lily full-blowing.

The dark eyes are liquidly starry
    As dew in the sun; and as tender
        Her voice as the harp of the breeze;
Such is the wood-lily's fairy,
    Such the magnolia's defender;
        She lives in the life of her trees,
And shines with the lily's white splendor.

Magnolia, the queen of the lilies,
    Spoke mildly to Mona, the maiden:

"I have answered thy call—I am here!
And well do I know what thy will is:
 Thou art pining and grieving, love-laden,
  For a false heart, unworthy a tear,
For a gift that thy whole life would sadden.

"But thou hast loved ever the forest,
 And therefore the wood-spirits love thee:
  The magic I will not refuse
That would bring back the youth thou adorest;
 But dark is the storm-cloud above thee!
  Pause, yet, in thy folly, and choose—
If earnest entreaties may move thee—

"Of two gifts we hold for thy choosing:
 The heart of a lover wide-ranging,
  A wingéd Love, light as the wind;
A gift where the winning is losing,
 The love of a mortal quick changing;
  A love that no shackles can bind,
No kindness can keep from estranging.

"But bright is the next gift we offer—
 A life and a being like ours!
  O take it, and with us rejoice!.
Bright the existence we proffer;
 Sweet is the life of the flowers!
  Take it—and blest be thy choice,
In the bliss of these bloom-laden bowers."

So spake the queen-lily; and, waving
    The emerald wand, at its lifting
        The flower-sprites came from the wood:
Sweet Lotis, the water-nymph, laving
    Her limbs in the water, slow-drifting
        Came, borne on the breast of the flood,
With pearls through her white fingers sifting.

The slim little spice-fay, Melissa,
    All bright in her necklace of coral;
        Clemátis, with snowy-white wreath;
The golden-haired fairy, Narcissa,
    And Ivybell, exquisite laurel;
        With Gladiole, dagger in sheath,
And Blanche, the sweet sprite of the sorrel—

The sprite of the sorrel-tree, whitest
    Of wood maidens, pale in her sweetness,
        Adorned with her delicate bells;
Green Holly, with coral-crown brightest;
    The laurels, in classic completeness;
        And, crowned with her pink-tinted cells,
Azalea, exact in her neatness:

Sweet Redbud, so gently inclining
    Her head with its purple-wreathed tresses;
        The Locust, with honey-sweet blooms:
Albrizzia, with silken locks shining;
    Acacia, whom sweetness oppresses;

Mimosa, whose sensitive plumes
Shrink back from the light wind's caresses.

Pomegranate, of blossoms most beauteous,
    And fruits of the rosiest blooming;
        Sweet Silverbell, whiter than snows;
And Orange, with berries bright-luteus,
    And breath the whole forest perfuming,
        And bridal-white garland, that shows
Through sprays of her foliage green-glooming.

All the flowers, from the Lily's pale beauty
    To Eglantine, lovely in blushes;
        All the tree-nymphs, in kirtles of green,
From the Tulip, who came to her duty
    As prompt as the smallest of bushes
        To lovely Chione serene,
Who bends her fair locks to the rushes.

The lily-queen spoke to the maiden:
    "Choose thou among these at thy pleasure,
        If thou wouldst be one of my train.
Thy spirit shall brighten and gladden,
    The sky shall grow softer in azure,
        And mountain, and forest and plain
Shall open to thee their hid treasure."

"If thou the sweet promise fulfillest,
    O spirit of beauty excelling!"
        Cried Mona, "to thee I will yield.

Give me *peace*—and the rest as thou willest!
    Choose *thou* my new floreal dwelling,
        From plants of the forest or field,
By stream or by fountain up-welling.

"Forever to dwell in this forest,
    This home of sweet visions enchanted!
        I ask, I entreat but for this!"
Then the queen : "If the past thou abhorrest,
    The future gives all thou hast wanted;
        It brings thee free gifts—all the bliss
    And affection for which thou hast panted."

"Then let it be mine to resemble,"
    Said Mona, "the blossom so tender
        She shrinks from the touch of the wind!
Mimosa, whose feather-leaves tremble,
    And quivering branches so slender;
        Like a shrinking and sensitive mind,
She bows in her timid surrender."

The lily-queen smiled, and the forest
    Grew bright with a magic illuming,
        And sweet was her breath on the breeze:
"I will give thee the gift thou implorest,
    And grant thee the power of assuming
        A form like the sensitive-trees
Around thee so lavishly blooming."

One touch from the wand of the fairy,
    And the maid, ere the eye could have missed her,
      Was gone—but a delicate vine
Was waving its feather-leaves airy
    With blooms of a silken-soft glister,
      The trailing mimosa—as fine
And as fair as her forest-born sister.

TO ALICE: A REVERIE.

(1864.)

When the faint fire-light flickers, red and lowly
    And evening winds are moaning at the pane;
When the dim hour of twilight, waning slowly,
    Is melancholy with a sound of rain—

Then Memory brings her jewel-girded chalice
    Whose magic draught recalls the days of old,
When, gifted with a Midas-touch, dear Alice,
    Youth's glowing fancy turned all things to gold.

Can you forget how once we sat together,
    While the pale twilight deepened into gloom,
And through the casement, in May's mildest weather,
    The sweet spring-breezes stole into the room?

We sat together, in the twilights olden,
    In the sweet rose time of enchanted youth;

The blue-eyed Rosa, with her tresses golden,
    Nannie the wise, and laughter-loving Ruth,

And auburn Alice, proud, yet gentle-hearted!—
    In these dark days of doubt, and grief, and pain,
How oft I think of these, the friends long parted!
    Youth's dawning-sun will never rise again.

Truly, I have lost idols, fondly cherished—
    Idols I could not think were made of clay;
But since those days, far higher hopes have perished,
    And dearer dreams since then have passed away.

I dream too much: and while thus idly musing
    On childish joys I cannot quite forget,
The present glides away, and I am losing
    Youth's sweeter roses, blooming for me yet.

Beholding *thy* bright face, my sad heart rallies:
    Speak to me—place your hand upon my brow,
And exorcise, with love's own touch, dear Alice,
    The brooding spirit that torments me now.

I trust you: though, too often, friendship human
    Is falsehood in disguise, I trust it yet!
You are, at least, true friend and peerless woman,
    Too wise to change, too faithful to forget.

ELIZABETH BARRETT BROWNING.

(May, 1865.)

"Crowned and buried," queenly dead!
    Sacred be thy place of rest;
Reverent be the silent tread
    Beside her grave we love the best;
And, if we speak, in praise or prayer,
Sweet be the tone that echoes there!

I loved thee from my earliest youth;
    I loved as only youth can love;
With all the fervor of the South;
    With steadfast faith that would not move:
By thee my spirit's depths were stirred,
As moonlight moves a mocking-bird.

A student in a busy school,
    I sat, with students all around:
The aspen-trees threw shadows cool
    Through the low window till they found
My seat beside the casement, where
My book-leaves rustled to the air.

In vain I read my lesson o'er:
    The absent spirit wandered free
With "Pan" upon the river shore;
    With "Margaret," and "Aurora Leigh;"

And through the open window played
The light and flickering aspen-shade.

I drank with thee the "Cyprus wine;"
    I saw "the Page" who loved so well;
I bowed before fair "Geraldine;"
    I heard the mournful passing-bell
That rang for "May" a deep refrain:
I stood with "Bertha in the Lane:"

I found the "Swan's-Nest" in the reeds:
    And heard the Star send mourning song
To Lucifer: "Onora's" beads—
    But wherefore count the unnumbered throng,
The shining shapes that follow thee,
Which all the world has loved with me!

I dreamed, in that sweet, simple time,
    That thou might'st look some future day,
Upon a humbler poet's rhyme,
    And, smiling, read my rustic lay,
An echo from green solitudes
In the bird-haunted Southern woods.

Thy loving Lord had need of thee:
    But from the world where now thou art,
Perchance thy spirit-eyes may see
    The hidden volume of my heart,
Reading its pages, one by one,
As I thy printed verse have done:

And thou those subtile chords canst see
    Which so my soul to thee did draw:
Thou knowest what thou wast to me,
    O friend, whose face I never saw!
Thou knowest how my childish soul
Was softened by thy sweet control!

The world has crowned thee with the bay,
    But I no classic wreath may twine;
A lily of the woods I lay
    Amid the laurels on thy shrine—
Magnolia, pure and perfect flower,
A type of sweetness blent with power.

THE SILK-TREE.

(1866.)

A slender tree, not high, nor branching wide;
    With supple boughs, and dainty leaves light-green;
And drooping from the boughs on every side,
    Long, lovely tassels wave their silken sheen;—

Pale-shining tassels, long, and soft and fair,
    And bright as corn-silk when the corn is young;
With hints of green, as on a mermaid's hair
    Faint shadows from her ocean-caves are flung.

Naiad of trees, the silk-tree loves dark dells,
    Where limpid streams in viny coverts hide,

Wherein the wild swamp-redbird* safely dwells,
  And ferns and trailing ivies grow beside.

The silk-tree bends her head above the brook,
  Like a fair maiden, beautiful and vain,
Who by some haunted streamlet paused to look,
  And never from the place might move again:

Because a water-witch, with jealous eyes,
  Changed the bright form and fixed forever there
The maiden's beauty in this green disguise—
  But spared her lovely locks of shining hair.

"IN DARKNESS AND THE SHADOW OF DEATH."

(August, 1868.)

Reapers, who lightly sowed the golden grain,—
  How thick their harvest-fields with goodly sheaves!
Others, who sowed in tears, and toiled in pain,
  For harvest have but weeds or barren leaves,
    And all their toil is vain.

The talent which Thou gavest to me, Lord,
  I buried not, nor hid away from sight,
Nor like a miser did my treasure hoard—
  But sought to use the costly gift aright,
    Obedient to thy word.

---

* "Swamp-redbird" is the local name for one of the Tanager family, noted for vividly scarlet plumage and almost untamable shyness and wildness.

Thine was the goodly seed, and thine the land,
   And thine the treasure; yet, I nothing earned!
So, when thy gifts Thou shalt again demand,
   I yield them gladly, lest all should be turned
      To evil, in my hand.

All Thou didst give to me to Thee I gave:
   Is it my fault that I can do no more?
Thy willing servant, not a sullen slave,
   Thine own to Thee I gladly do restore,
      And no reward would crave.

O righteous God, who holy art and true!
   O Christ the Lord, who lowly wast and meek!
Show me the work that Thou wouldst have me do;
   Omnipotence! have mercy on the weak,
      And my spent strength renew.

O Thou the Strong, break not the bruiséd reed!
   O Thou the Good, look not upon my ill!
All-Perfect Thou; and I am frail, indeed!
   Help me thy gracious pleasure to fulfill;
      Grant me the help I need.

My errors and my ignorance, forgive;
   Unprofitable, yet, Thy servant still!
Or, if Thou canst not pardon, yet reprieve;
   And if I am too weak to do Thy will,
      Unfit Thy life to live—

Unfit for earth, and more unfit for heaven,—
   In all Thy universe is there no place
For weary souls, uncursed though unforgiven?—
   Foiled in the fight and distanced in the race,
      Thou knowest, I have striven.

Unfit for Thy pure Presence, which has blessed
   The conquering hosts, the sainted souls sublime;
Helpless and blind, unknowing what is best,
   A driven leaf upon the storm of Time,—
      I pray Thee, Lord, for rest.

MUSIC IN THE NIGHT.

(June, 1875.)

My head was full of pain, my heart of grief;
   Sultry the summer night, and close the room:
I threw the casement open for relief,
   And stood there, gazing out on kindred gloom.

Night caused, at least, the clamorous sounds to cease
   That all day long rose from the busy street:
I strove to utter thanks for night and peace—
   But night and peace no more to me were sweet.

The moon was up, and through the trees she sped
   A slender shaft, that touched my breast with light;
And, suddenly I heard, above my head,
   Ethereal music flowing through the night.

Ethereal-fine as any wind-harp's note:
    Eolian music, but no breath of wind!
Was it a browny's bugle far remote,
    Or prairie-spirit, piping to his kind?

Could it be fairy-flute or pixy-shell,
    Or harp of some sweet elfin-of-the-light?
An Ariel's tabor, or the crystal bell
    Swung by a sylph lone-singing in the night?

Who was the sweet musician, all unseen?
    Faint grew the sounds, receding to the skies:
Was it some gentle genie's tamborine,
    Or wandering Peri, seeking Paradise?

Far out I leaned, and looked up in the sky,
    Half fancying I might catch the vanishing
Of sprite or angel;—but, the melody
    Came from a small bird, singing on the wing.

It was my childhood's joy, the mocking-bird,
    Whose song I scarce had hoped to hear again;
It was the Southern nightingale I heard,
    Singing to Western skies his rapturous strain.

Upon the moonlit air he lightly hung,
    Waving his wings in time to his own tune;
Then floated up, and up, and ever sung,
    As if he rose to meet the listening moon.

And while, entranced in silent joy, I drank
   The melting sadness of the distant sound,
Down from the sky he swiftly, softly sank,
   In long, smooth sweeps, until he touched the ground,

Whence, instant, up he sprang in spiral flight,
   Changing the liquid sweetness of his strain
To wild, exultant rapture of delight;
   And stronger, clearer, wilder, the refrain.

And up he circled, upward, upward, still;
   Then, down, and up, and round, and round once more;
While clear, and sweet, and wild, and liquid-shrill,
   The strong, triumphant joy did he out-pour.

At last, in rapid circles, he descends
   Upon a cedar's top; his shrilling note
More softly cadenced, till the pean ends
   With a low, liquid gurgle in his throat:

Ends for a space, that he may swing and sway—
   Then comes a sudden burst of mimicry;
From branch to branch he flits, from spray to spray,
   From bower to chimney, and from roof to tree.

Anon, the moon's exhilarating light
   Inspires the witching melody he sings:
If sounds had hues, the song were pearly white
   As the sweet moon that gilds his restless wings.

And so, through cadenced falls, the music glides
    Into a silver sound of tenderest tone,
Like the low lapsing of moon-lighted tides
    On some enchanted beach or islet lone.

The smooth, sweet notes are full of peace and rest:
    They steal like drops of healing through the ear;
They drop like balm on tired brain and breast,
    Till the rapt hearer only breathes to hear.

Entranced, I stood, when, rising like a stream,
    The song, with one high, thrilling note long-drawn,
Ceased suddenly:—I woke, as from a dream;
    And through the window came the golden dawn.

ONE IN TEN.

(Jan. 4, 1876.)

Why do you weep and wail,
    And talk of ingratitude?
Your tears will not avail
    To change the worldling's mood,
    Nor make the evil good,
Though you weep till the stars grow pale.

This lesson is set for all:
    They gave you stones for bread;
For honey, they gave you gall;
    For wine, they poured instead

The bitter juices shed
From the wild grape's poisonous ball.

Remember—in days gone by
  Ten lepers stood in the way,
Waiting till Christ came nigh:
    Ghastly and gaunt were they;
    The helpless, hopeless prey
Of the hideous leprosy.

Far off they stood, and cried
  To the Lord of life and death;
Nor was their prayer denied:
    "Depart!" the Saviour saith,
    "In my healing Word have faith,
And ye shall be purified."

The Master's grace restored
  Health to those haggard men;
Life and health, at his word,
    Throbbed in their pulses again:
    And, yet—but one of the ten
Came back to thank the Lord.

Only one soul discerned
  The false life from the true;
Only the stranger returned
    Of all that thankless crew:—
    Will the world keep faith with *you*,
When the Lord of Life was spurned?

INDIAN SUMMER.*

(October 22, 1856.)

'Tis now the Indian summer, each leaf of varied hue
Is wearing, every changing hour, a color bright and new.
Tall maples, with their crimson leaves; the oak, of regal red;
The poplar, with his yellow plume, waves loftily his head.

And pines, with dark, unchanging green, their aid in contrast lend;
While scattered leaves from other trees their mingled colors blend:
So thickly and so bright they lie, all scattered by the way,
As if the spring had come again, with all her blossoms gay.

Each oak† and sumac-leaf might be a rose without perfume,
The painted sassafras excels a tulip's varied bloom:
And others, deep in hollows dark, lie withered, dry and sear,
Sad emblems of our fading lives, the warnings of the year.

---

*Preserved because it was the first published poem of the author, written at a very early age, (as it shows in itself;) so early, indeed, as often to elicit *doubts* of so young a child's ability to think in rhyme, notwithstanding many well known cases of more extreme precocity. So much by way of apology for the author's eldest born and (*therefore*) favorite brain-child.

†" *Oak-leaf,*" i. e , the Spanish-oak leaf: the poem was written in a grove of Spanish oaks.

A COMPARISON.

TO ALICE.

(July 21, 1876.)

Your life is like a summer stream
    Embosomed in a flowery wood;
There, falls no scorching noonday gleam,
    No careless footsteps there intrude:
But mine—a mountain-torrent brave;
    Swollen with floods of wild spring-rain,
Yet conscious of a broader wave,
    And stronger when it smiles again.

Your heart is like a sensitive-vine:
    Torn from its dear familiar ties,
Round new supports it will not twine,
    But droops its beauteous wreath, and dies.
But mine—the trailing-ivy shoot;
    Uprooted, broken, tossed aside,
Trampled to earth—it takes fresh root,
    And spreads its leaves in greener pride.

DISCONTENT.

(1862.)

I.

Into her little room she goes,
    And through the open window there
She breathes the fragrance of the rose
    And feels the west-wind move her hair.

The day is gone, her task is done;
    Until to-morrow's sun shall rise
The dews of sleep may fall upon
    Her tired limbs and aching eyes.

She lingers, ere she goes to rest,
    Leaning upon the window-sill:
The moon shows palely in the East,
    The dew is on the airy hill.

The sun is nearly out of sight,
    But pours his radiance in a flood
Of golden gleams and rosy light,
    Flaming behind the western wood.

That golden-glowing West appears
    Like some bright Eden-land afar;
Against it, every tree-trunk rears
    A black line, like a prison-bar.

"I know the charm will fade," she said,
    "Like fairy gold; the glamour goes,

And from the West the light has fled,
    And drops of twilight bend the rose.

I know, beneath the Western sky
    Those Eden-lands are common grounds;
Yet I would go—and freely *die*,
    Once having burst these prison-bounds!"

2.

She walked across the dewy lawn;
    The house was wrapped in slumber still:
She watched the coming of the dawn,
    Above the green, dew-shining hill.

The birds in liquid snatches sung,
    And whistled with a mellow sound;
The wind swept through her flowers and flung
    The full-blown petals on the ground.

She murmured: "Was the poet right,
    Whose words so oft I lingered o'er,
That 'beauty is a joy,' a light
    To cheer the mind forevermore?

"*I* have no joy: the fields are fair,
    The winds play through the rustling trees;
Sweet murmurs fill the fragrant air—
    And, yet, I have no joy in these!

"The sameness wearies all my soul:
    I have so often gazed upon

These valleys, where the mists uproll,
    Bright silver-purple in the sun:

"And I have walked among my flowers,
    And wandered in the deep-green wood,
Till I could count the languid hours
    By the unfolding of a bud.

"The prison-shadow covers me:
    My heart is sad, my life is dull:
I have no joy in aught I see—
    And yet the world is beautiful!"

"FANNIE."

(To F. B., *of Virginia, and* F. E., *of Texas.)*

"What's in a name?" Not very much, in sooth,
    And yet, a name can wake our love or hate:
    I like to hear the cordial sound of KATE,
Of gentle ADA, and of simple RUTH:
MARY flows liquidly, and pure, and smooth,
    A name at once to love and venerate,
    And well I love the modest name sedate
Of ALICE, charming synonym of truth:
But, FANNIE, what to thee shall I compare?
    The dew on blossoms, in the summer's heat!

So pure, so bright, so tender, and so fair,
   In every maiden charm and grace complete,
Are they who this soft appellation wear—
   The TWO who make the name of FANNIE sweet.

FIDELITY.

TO ALICE.

(Jan. 1, 1877.)

I called thee "faithful friend and woman peerless,"
   In our first youth: twelve changing years are gone,
But *thou* hast never changed; fond, faithful, fearless;
   Surely, of women born the noblest one.

What words can image thee, the true and tender,
   Large-brained, warm-hearted, proud, yet sweet and kind?
All meaner beauty pales its earthly splendor
   Before thy loveliness of heart and mind.

Others, indeed, have virtues, and have graces;
   Each has some separate gift, but *thou* hast *all!*
Virtue with virtue, grace with grace inlaces,
   Weaving for thee a perfect coronal.

Women there are as loving and as gentle,
   And women there may be as worthy trust;
But, who, as thou, blends moral strength with mental,
   Loyal as loving, generous as just?

"Sensitive-vine," I called thee, for thy sweetness,
   Thy true refinement, fond fidelity;
But no one flower can image in completeness
   That strong, bright soul: there is no type of thee!

I quarrel not with Fate! she sent pale malice,
   Envy, and hate, my shrinking soul to rend,
But, to make full amends, she gave me ALICE—
   Another name for life's best gift, a friend.

MY BROTHER.

(1876.)

Alas! my brother, thou, to whom I sung
   In dawning youth,
Thou, who didst walk with me the paths among
   Those flower-sweet woodlands of our native South—

Little I dreamed that Death must soon lay low
   That bright, young head!
How bright, and how beloved, those only know
   Whose star of life went out when thou wert dead.

The Western wind sweeps freely o'er thy grave,
   But days may come
When the sweet Southern fringetree there may wave,
   And the wild iris cluster purple bloom;

And passion-flowers shall cling about a cross
  Above thee raised,
And virgin lilies, set in emerald moss—
  For thou didst love the lilies Jesus praised.

"THE LIGHT OF OTHER DAYS."

(1879.)

We were three happy children in one dwelling;
  Our eldest brother—ah! so long ago!—
We two obeyed, the law of love compelling,
  And followed in his footsteps to and fro.

And we thought nothing of his patient kindness,
  No more than of the sun, the vital air:
His tender care we took with happy blindness,
  Deeming that love and trust were everywhere.

The marsh-magnolia, queen of Piedmont forests,
  We stripped of long leaves, green as malachite;
And her great lilies, to the little florists,
  Seemed perfumed vases for Queen Mab's delight.

We broke, for silvan parasols to shade us,
  Magnolia-boughs, around whose tips were whorled
Those long leaves, one of which, when folded, made us
  The sweetest drinking-cup in all the world.

The mocking-bird sang to the summer roses,
  And then the lily-trees their blossoms shed;

But, later when the passion-flower uncloses,
    The marsh-magnolia pods are rosy red.

The Indian-arrow blazed in autumn splendor
    When the new-ripened nuts we gathered in:
We made the wintergreen its fruit surrender,
    And shook in shining showers the chinquapin.

You ask—why things so childish I remember?
    An empty shell keeps murmuring of the sea;
A thought of fire is in the coldest ember—
    And the lone spirit lives in memory.

SERENADE.

FOR FANNIE.

(June, 1874.)

The star of twilight glows, love,
    Lone-shining in the blue;
The flowers of night unclose, love,
    Beneath the gathering dew:
While night is softly stealing
    Over the liquid sea,
Half veiling, half revealing—
    I'll tune my harp to thee.

The stars that fill the skies, love,
    Their silent vigils keep

Until the moon shall rise, love,
  Out of the trembling deep—
And while the moon is glancing
  Over the sparkling sea,
Its glories all enhancing—
  My song shall be of thee.

"ROSA SENZA SPINAS."

In memory of J. S. S., *of Danville, Va.*

O lovely and belovéd! Whitest rose,
  Pearl-shining with the sweetest dews of morn!
  Full-hearted rose, that never knew a thorn!
Death shuts thy petals ere the morning goes.
And it is better so: no winter snows
  Can chill thee, in thy summer beauty borne
  From earth to heaven, ere thou hadst learned to mourn,
As all earth's children must, denied repose,
  Which men call death: sweet is the tender call
Of Death to Youth, and soonest heard by those
  Nearest to heaven, brightest and best of all:
And where the stream of life through Eden flows,
This folded flower shall all its leaves unclose,
  In perfect bloom, that shall not fade nor fall.

THE FAIRY RING.

(1877.)

I walked the forest, in midsummer days,
    Indulging idlest dreams and wildest fancies,
Musing along the lovely woodland ways,
    With aimless steps, absorbed in blissful trances.

And there I saw, within the forest dim,
    A tiny, winding path, distinctly threading
A maze of inter-tangling vine and limb,
    And eglantine with thorny branches spreading.

This pretty little path was smooth and green
    With moss, and ferny fringes marked the border,
While tall trees overhead had thrown a screen
    As thick as ever grew to nature's order.

The path emerged from tangled vine and fern,
    And spice, and pink azalea, thickly growing
About a marsh, where rank, red blossoms burn,
    And Indian-arrow drops its berries glowing.

What foot could penetrate that marshy brake?
    What daring hand those woven vines could sever,
Nor fear to rouse the spotted water-snake,
    Nor start to feel the treacherous quicksand quiver?

Stooping, I saw a narrow bridge of moss
    Away into the marshy tangle winding:

It seemed to bridge the sluggish stream across,
    But whither then it went, was past my finding.

Turning, I followed it into the gloom
    Of the rose-thicket where I first espied it;
To walk that narrow path I had small room,
    So close the tangling vines had grown beside it.

But, having passed the thicket, larger space
    There was: the mossy pathlet, curving, twisting,
Through ranks of silver birches, reached a place
    As sweet as ever saw a fairy's trysting.

It was a moss-grown opening in the wood,
    A little dell, much like a round, green dimple
Of Mother Earth; and in the center stood
    A small, round, placid spring, without a rimple;

As if a silver basin had been placed
    For some fair dryad's bath of fragrant waters,
Or like some fallen mirror, which had graced
    The airy tiring-room of cloudland's daughters.

There was no outlet to this placid well,
    At least none visible: it lay as quiet
As a great gleaming dewdrop in the dell,
    Reflecting ferns and blossoms that grew by it.

Around were groups of water-loving trees,
    The fringe-tree, and the beautiful cucumber,

The glistening laurel, and, more frail than these,
    Fairy mimosas, drooping as in slumber.

O'er all the dell there shone the tender light
    Of dying day: the moon had risen early,
And through the forest-trees upon the right,
    Shot long, straight lines of light, like lances pearly

Touching the soft green mosses of the dell.
    And the fair trees that grew as in a garden;—
Surprise and pleasure bound me like a spell!
    So small a park should have a fairy warden.

I still stood in that small, green path that led
    To this sweet pleasure-plot; and there it ended:
The forest-trees met dark above my head,
    Great oaks, with mistletoe in wreaths suspended.

And looking down before me, I could see
    A fairy ring, my onward steps opposing;
A fringe of grass, that circled all the lea,
    The little dell in magic bounds inclosing.

Aloud I spoke, half earnest, half in sport:
    "Oh, would I had the fated four-leaf clover,
So I might look upon the fairy court,
    And step, unharmed, the magic circle over."

And, speaking thus, I looked upon the ring,
    Whose tall, rank grasses seemed to part and waver:

I saw a four-leaf clover forward swing—
    I saw, and stooped, and plucked the fairy favor;

And then, the fairy ring I stepped within :—
    There came a silver sound of fairy laughter,
And small, sweet voices made a merry din,
    And tripping feet and whirring wings came after.

They hung like flights of butterflies in air,
    They sprang like fire-flies from the dewy grasses;
They rode by troops on elfin coursers fair;
    They flashed like wild-fire from the dark morasses.

With clasping hands, the fairy boys and girls
    Kept time in airy dances, circling, swinging,
Brighter than roses wreathed, or strings of pearls;
    And all the wood re-echoed to their singing,

To sound of pipe and tabor, lute and shell,
    And golden harp, and silver flute entrancing:
And as the waves of music rose and fell,
    So rose and fell the airy circles dancing.

Then did the fountain, swelling high and higher,
    While all its troubled water whirls and darkles,
Shoot upward in a jet of silver fire,
    Descending in a rain of starry sparkles.

And laughing water-fairies, small and bright,
    Rode on the tossing jets of silver-burning;

Now flashing skyward in a stream of light,
    And now in rainbow-tinted spray returning.

But, oh! the queen—the fairest of the fair!
    Robe, silver gauze, with diamonds all a twinkle;
A starry crown upon her floating hair,
    That caught the light on every golden crinkle.

A waxen calla-lily, pure as snow,
    Formed the queen's car: six humming-birds before her
Drew on the chariot, and, in regal show,
    A purple passion-flower was carried o'er her,

Borne by a winged sprite for a canopy
    To shade Titania's eyes of starry azure;
And, on each side, a brilliant butterfly
    Fanned her with wings that waved in rhythmic measure:

Those gorgeous bird-flies,* bearing colors bright
    As humming-birds upon their jeweled winglets;
And fire-flies round her wove a web of light,
    Bright-sparkling as the diamonds in her ringlets.

A ring of fairies flew on every side
    Around their lovely mistress, to attend her,
And warbling orioles, redbirds, bluebirds, vied
    With many more, in pride of plumy splendor.

---

* "Bird-flies;" that is, those beautiful butterflies that, in their shape and brilliant coloring strongly resemble humming-birds. Science knows them by another name than that of *bird-fly*, or *tobacco-fly*, the beautiful pest of Virginia planters.

The mockbird sang incessant, and in showers
    Came down the summer-dew invigorating,
Till, at their queen's approach, the laughing flowers
    Gave out a fragrance half intoxicating.

Wild with delight, I quite forgot myself:
    I clapped my hands—and dropped the four-leaf clover!
Instant, the lights were out, and every elf
    Melted like mist: the fairy dream was over!

THE JEWEL-SEEKER.

Addressed to Mrs. L. R. M., *of Kansas City, Mo.*

A child once dreamed he saw an angel fair,
    Holding a gem, whence light like star-beams spread,
Soft-luminous. "Seek thou this jewel rare;
    Seek it through all the world!" the angel said.

Next day, the child saw dew-drops in the sun,
    And thought the jewel shone in one of them;
But, when he plucked the grasses, one by one
    Dropped down and vanished every liquid gem.

Yet, still he sought the jewel, year by year,
    Through happy childhood and a youth of dreams:
He searched deep mines, and mountain-caverns drear,
    And ocean-depths, and beds of limpid streams.

So earnestly the seeker longed to find
    This charmèd jewel of supernal light,
That sweet delusion fell upon his mind,
    And common things grew precious in his sight.

Oft-times, he treasured bits of colored glass,
    Pebbles, and painted shells, for jewels rare :
But, when he put them to the proof, alas!
    He found the wondrous jewel was not there.

And men said, mournfully, the gem he sought
    Illumined earth no longer with its beam :
But others mocked; and said the gem was naught
    But the bright fancy of a poet's dream.

The jewel seeker could not think it so,
    Yet, hoped no more to find this rarest stone :
But he had found, in seeking to and fro,
    Strange things and fair, which else he had not known.

Then came the angel of his dream once more :
    "Thou hast been faithful to thy task, and learned
The lesson well! Look now upon thy store
    Of common things, and see what thou hast earned."

Behold, among the pebbles in his hand
    One flashed in rainbow tint and starry ray!
The jewel he had sought through sea and land
    Had come to him disguised as common clay.

" *One* priceless gem," the angel said, "is thine,
    Won by thy faith—but *this* I bring thee, see!
Is a free gift of the great Power Divine,
    Who sends this second jewel unto thee!"

O friend beloved, thou joy of Heaven's bestowing!
    I thought myself most rich in *one* such gem :
But Friendship fills my cup to overflowing,
    And crowns me with her brightest diadem.

THE MOCKING-BIRD.

(June, 1875.)

Leaning upon my balcony, I feel
The subtile breath of twilight round me steal,
And from the garden that beneath me lies
O'errun with bloom, the mingling odors rise.
Smooth-rolling from the distant garden-beds
In grassy verdure sweep the level meads;
Beyond, the woody hill-tops meet the sky,
And, at their foot, a river flowing by.
Forever wails, upon the distant hill,
The twilight bird, the boding whippowil;
Forever from the garden-bower is heard
The throbbing cadence of the mocking-bird.

    " *Whip-po-wil!*"

"Light lingers, still!
Beauty is on the green hill-side,
    And coolness in the shade !
Up from the river clear and wide
The full tones of the rippling tide
    Roll musical and glad :
Where, gliding soft with murmuring roll
    The river ripples by,
Upon each greenly-rising knoll,
Like memories on a weary soul,
    The gathered shadows lie."

    "*Whip-po-wil!*"

The garden is a tangled waste of flowers,
Intricate walks, and thickly-shaded bowers :
Tuberose and jasmine blend their odors there,
And the rich roses blossom everywhere;
The winding walks are strewed with silver sand,
And fringed with flowering plants on either hand;
Sweet heliotropes, and starry asphodels;
Myrtles; and fuchsias, trailing crimson bells;
Lilies of many colors, golds, and blues,
And orange shades, and rich vermilion hues;
But sweetest are the lilies virgin-white,
Set in broad leaves as green as malachite.
Trailing-mimosa clasps the garden bower,
With yellow-jasmine twined, and passion-flower.
Whatever tree, or shrub, or flower is fair,

What vine is graceful, grows and blossoms there:
The whole bright landscape in the moonlight lies,
Fair as a lingering dream of Paradise.
"*Whip-po-wil!*"

                      "The world is still!
Sleep, weary world; forget thy weariness!
Sleep, cruelty, forgetting to oppress!
O eyes that ache, that only wake to weep!
O hearts that break, forget—forget in sleep!"
"*Whip-po-wil!*"

                      Ah, boding bird, be still!
I would not hear thy mournful monotone,
But listen to the mocking-bird alone.
Sweet mocking-bird, winged music of the woods,
Interpreter of varying Nature's moods,
Thou, who hast learned in moonlight solitudes
To blend in one full song all sounds of bliss,—
The whippowil hath made thee sing amiss,
And all thy music deepens into pain:
But, sing, sweet mocking-bird! sing now again,
And from thy mellow throat the music pour
Of hope, and joy, and beauty evermore.

    "I sing to the bride of the night,
      To the tuberose, loved of the night,
Who holds her fragrant breath the long day through;
    The flower most exquisite.

The flower of all delight,
Who opens her heart to the night,
To the night, and the silence, and dew.
O type of the faithful few!
O type of the fond and the true,
Who can love when the light of joy is gone,
When the day of happiness is done—
As the tuberose breathes her heart alone
To the night, and silence, and dew."
"*Whip-po-will!*"

The bird of twilight still
Calls from his covert on the crested hill,
But the sweet mocking-bird has drawn more near,
And from the orange-tree arises clear
His liquid note, that flows like molten gold:
A song of youth, and pleasures manifold.

"I sing from the scented orange-tree;
I sing a song of memory;
And by the deep-green orange-tree
The rich pomegranate grows,
And near them both, abundantly
Blossoms the royal rose.
I sing of the days gone by,
The dream-led days of youth!
I sing of enchanted lands that lie
In light beneath life's morning-sky,

All bright with the rose-empurpled dye
    Of the beautiful dawn of youth!
    And the visions of youth again
    Awake to my wild, sweet strain;
    They come in a shining train
        From the bloom-laden land of the South;
They bring thee a draught divine,
Sweeter and stronger than wine,—
A draught from the fountains of Youth, that shine
        Afar in the radiant South!"

The dark-blue sky has changed to amethyst;
The tender clouds are fine as melting mist;
And in the morn's full glory, plain are seen
The garden's varied hues, the meadow's green.
Sing, mocking-bird, interpret Nature's bliss!
That silver song becomes a night like this.
"*Whip-po-wil!*"
        "The night is still!
The risen moon is high above the hill;
The meads are bright with lavish light,
The melting mist is pearly white,
And heaven smiles on earth to-night,
        Tranced in the silence of light!
        Trembling to the beams,
Glancing, glittering, go the starry streams;
The river like a jeweled girdle gleams,
And like a thread of twisted silver seems
        The little meadow-rill;—

The curving, crinkling, silver-twinkling, faintly-
tinkling meadow-rill!"
"*Whip-po-wil!*"

Heavy with perfume droops the languid breeze,
Yet moves, as if to subtle harmonies:
Beauty and melody and fragrance make
The swooning sense with over-sweetness ache;
The roses quiver, and the lilies shake,
And the whole garden moves, as if it stirred
To the wild music of the mocking-bird.

"The dews of night are shed
On the regal roses red,
On the silver lilies, gleaming through the dark;
And the moon's white splendor shines
On the clustering passion-vines,
Till every clinging drop of dew becomes a diamond spark.
The fringèd blossoms sway
As the winds about them play,
And the trembling dew-drops fall, a fairy shower;
The diamond droplets fall
From her purple coronal,
From the fairest flower of all, the peerless passion-flower!
O flower of night and morn!
O crown beset with thorn!
A type of helpless pain, a type of kingly power!
Of all the blossoms born
Earth's bosom to adorn,

Most beautiful, most dear art thou, imperial passion-
      flower!"

The dewy blossoms glisten as they bend, and sway and
      listen!

"O soul of the poet, be strong!
I will sing thee a sweeter song
Than all I have sung thee before,
Than the songs that I sung thee of yore:

"When earth is past
    With its bale and its bliss,
Forgotten, at last,
    Like the nothing it is,—
When the pain that is o'er
    Has taught thee, at length,
That meekness is power,
    And weakness is strength—

"The Giver of all thy loved will recall,
    And all thy lost treasures restore:
    And the wine of life will pour,
    Till thy shallow cup run o'er,
    And the red wine fall to the floor.
Listen—listen—listen to my golden song once more!

" There is meaning full and clear
For a poet's dreaming ear,

In my song without a word;
A song of a hope deferred;
A song of a race that is run;
A song of a new day begun;
A song of the South and the sun—
A song of the mocking-bird!"